THE STANTHORPE FLOODS QUEENSLAND 2021 AND 2022

BEFORE, DURING AND AFTER THE FLOODS

ADELAIDE MEHARG

Copyright © 2022 by Adelaide Meharg. 845037

All rights reserved. No part of this book may be reproduced or transmitted in any form or by any means, electronic or mechanical, including photocopying, recording, or by any information storage and retrieval system, without permission in writing from the copyright owner.

To order additional copies of this book, contact:
Xlibris
AU TFN: 1 800 844 927 (Toll Free inside Australia)
AU Local: 02 8310 8187 (+61 2 8310 8187 from outside Australia)
www.xlibris.com.au
Orders@Xlibris.com.au

ISBN:	Softcover	978-1-6698-3145-7
	EBook	978-1-6698-3146-4

Print information available on the last page

Rev. date: 08/22/2022

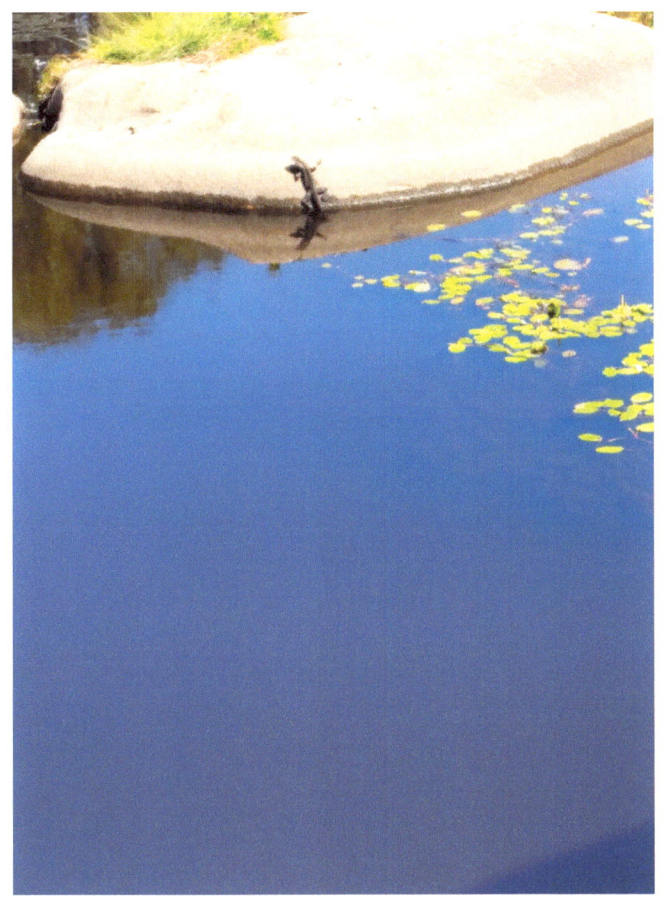
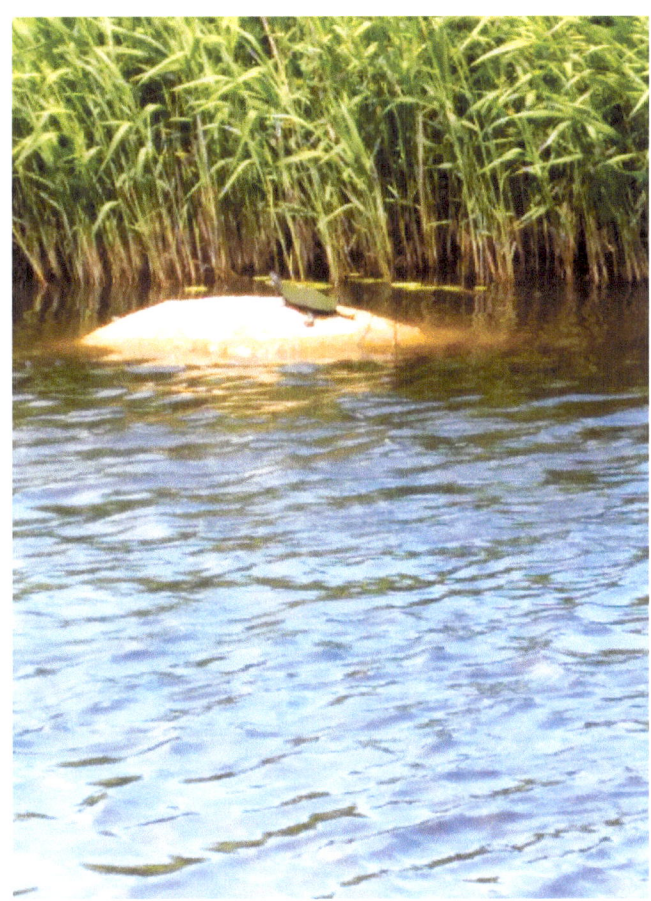
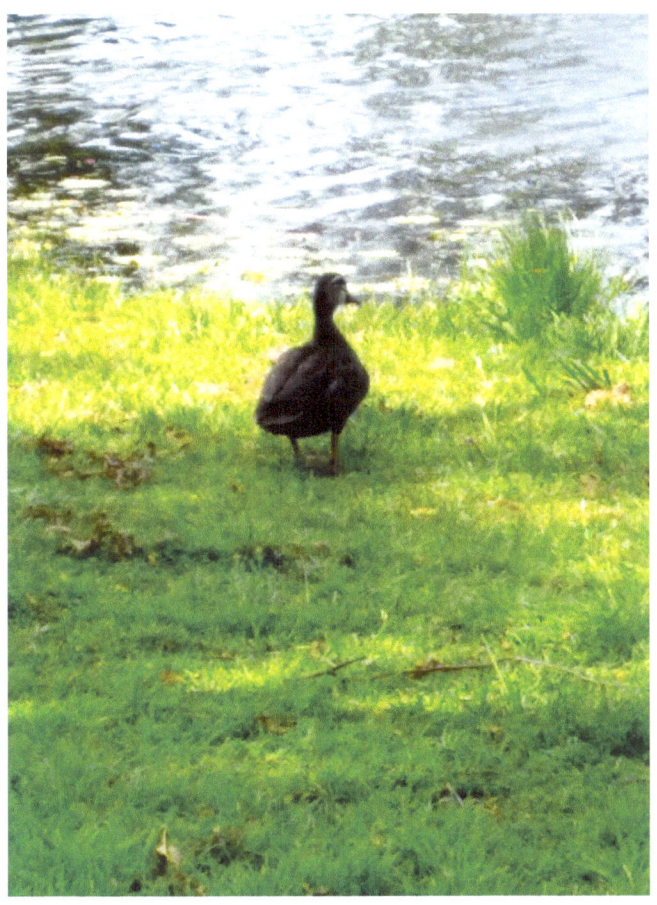
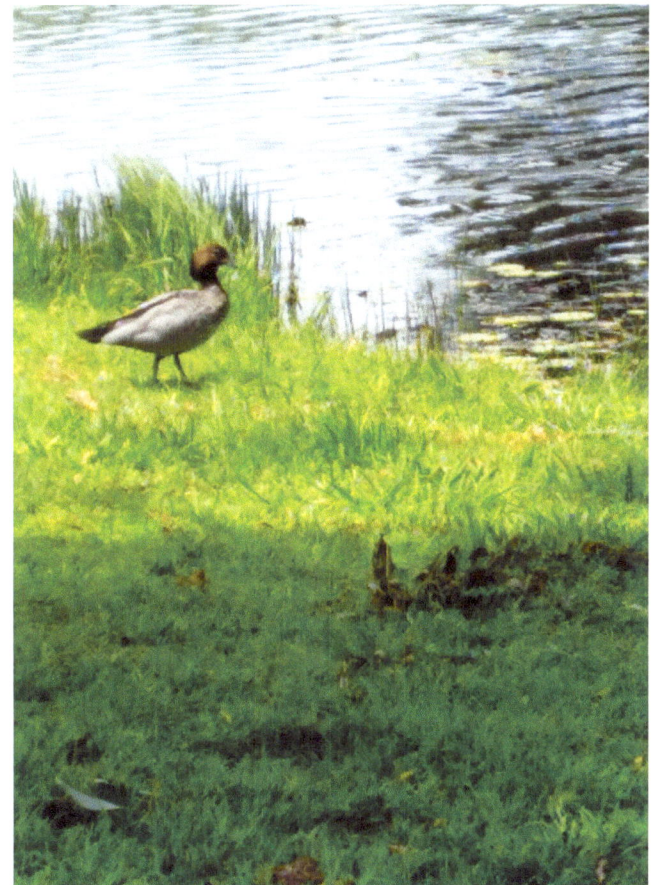

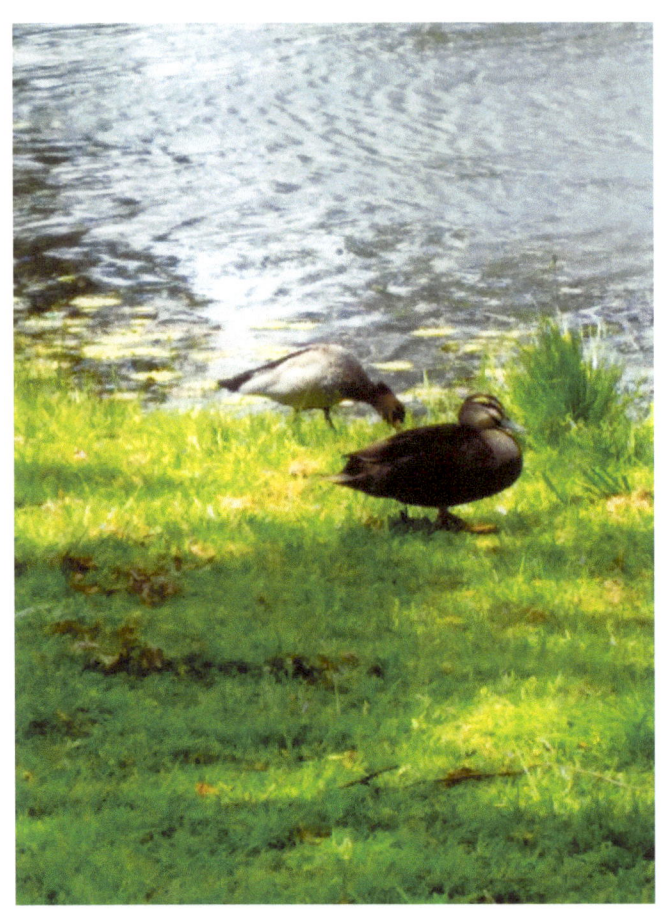
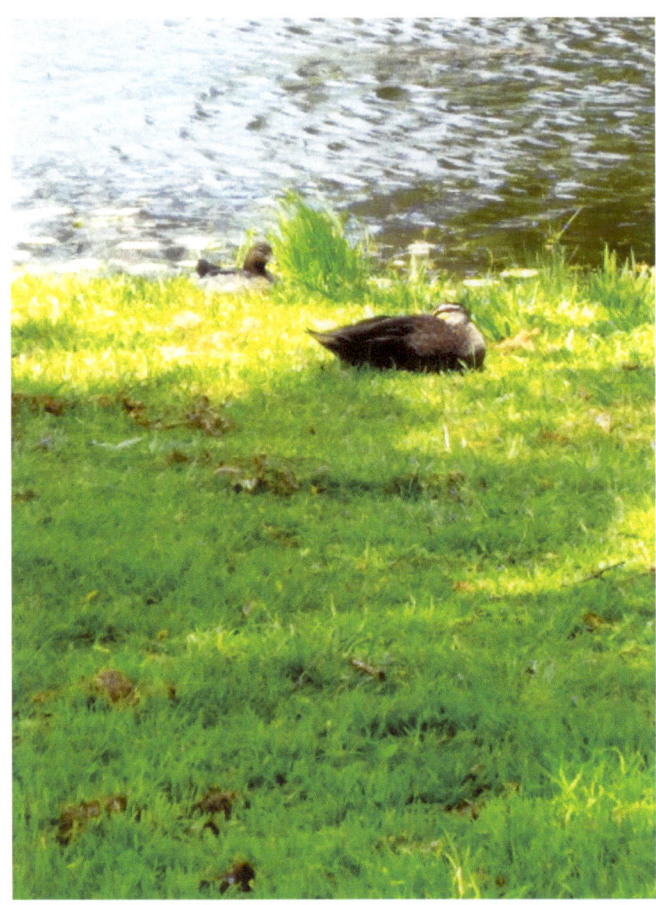
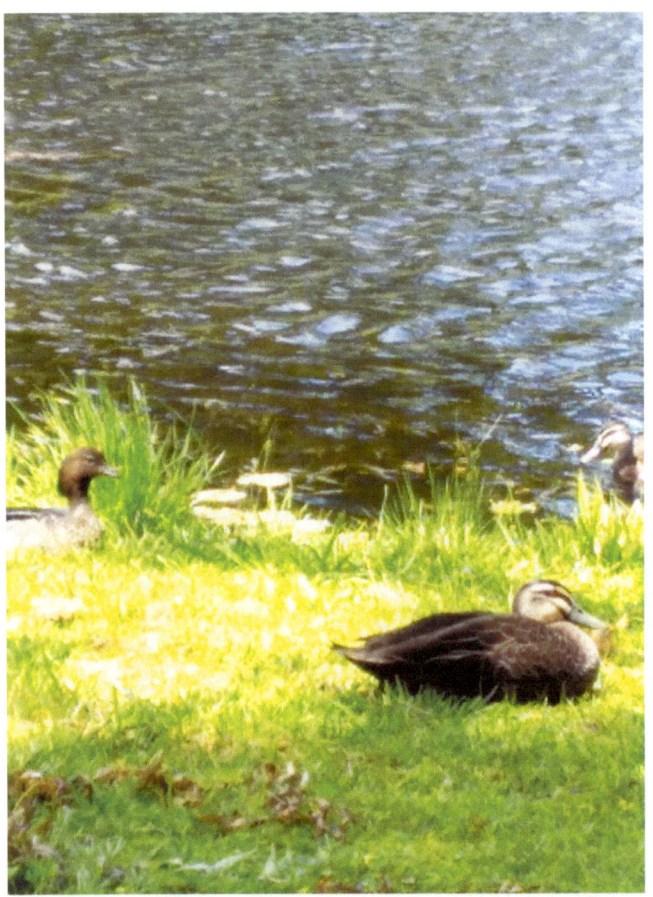
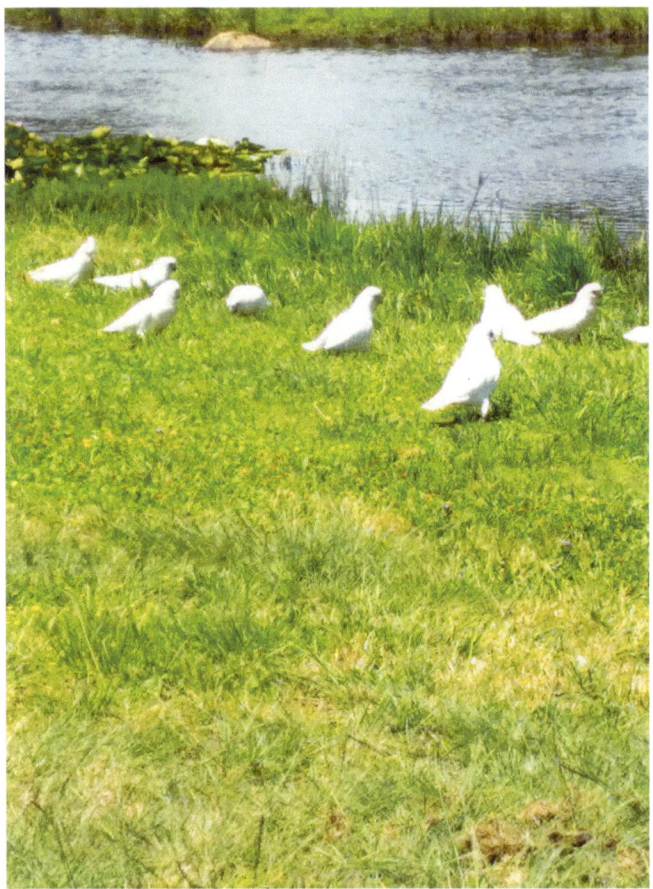

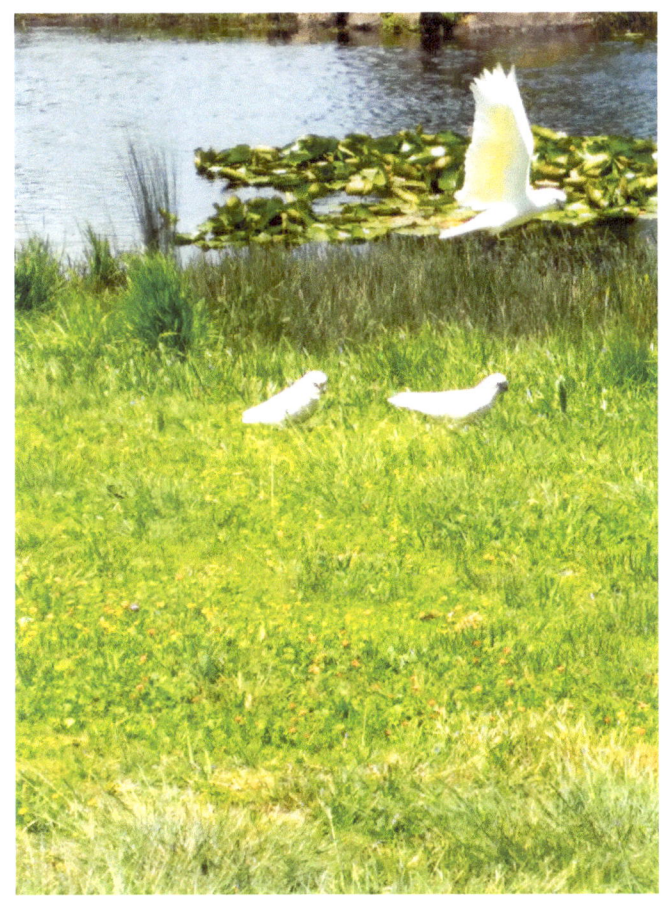
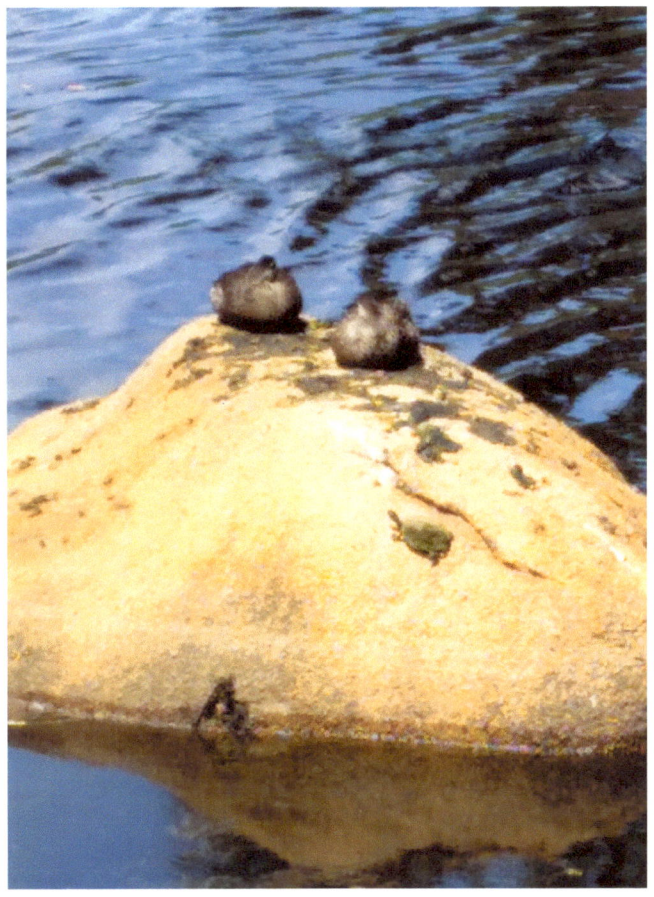
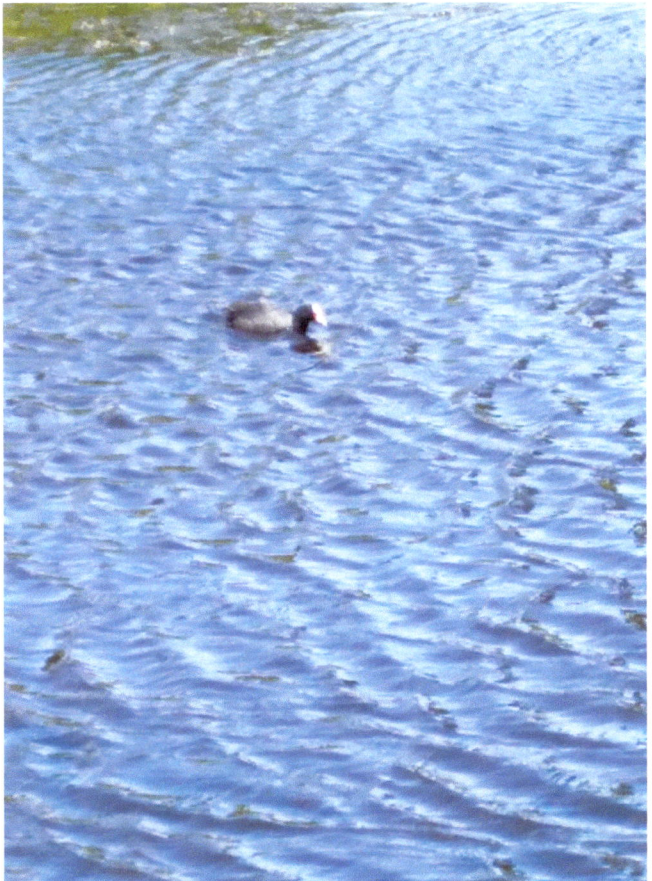
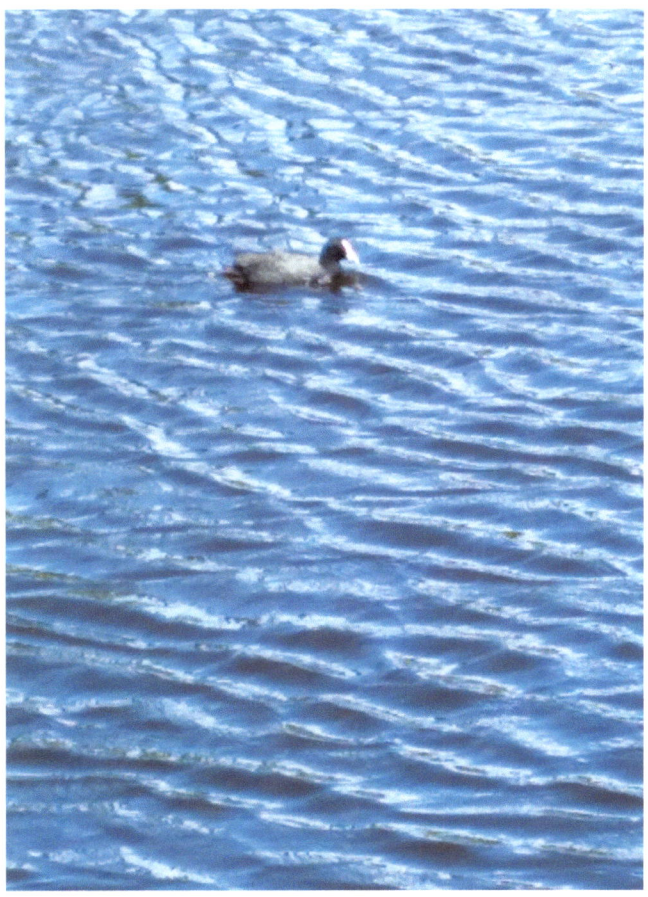

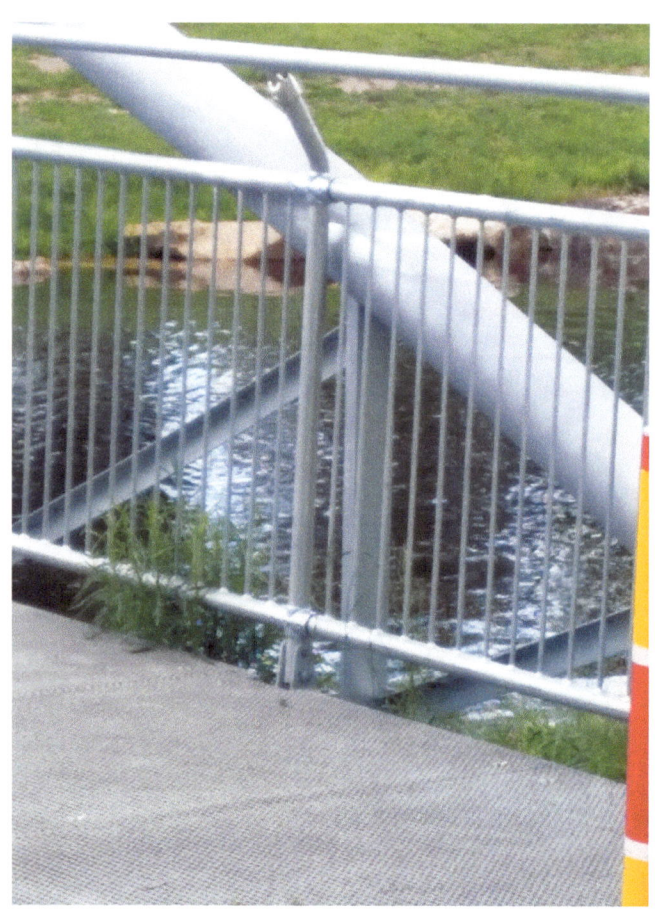
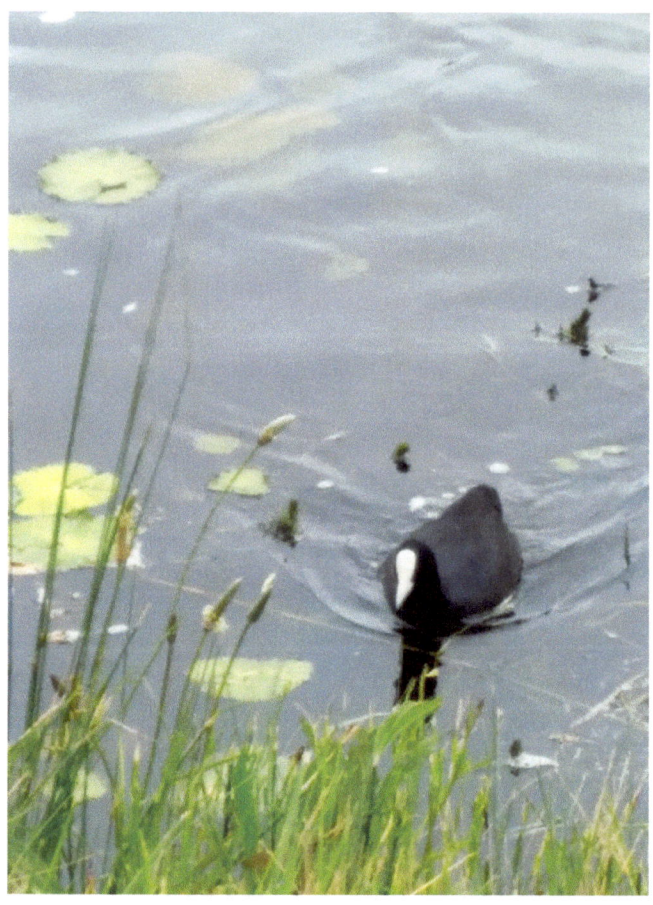
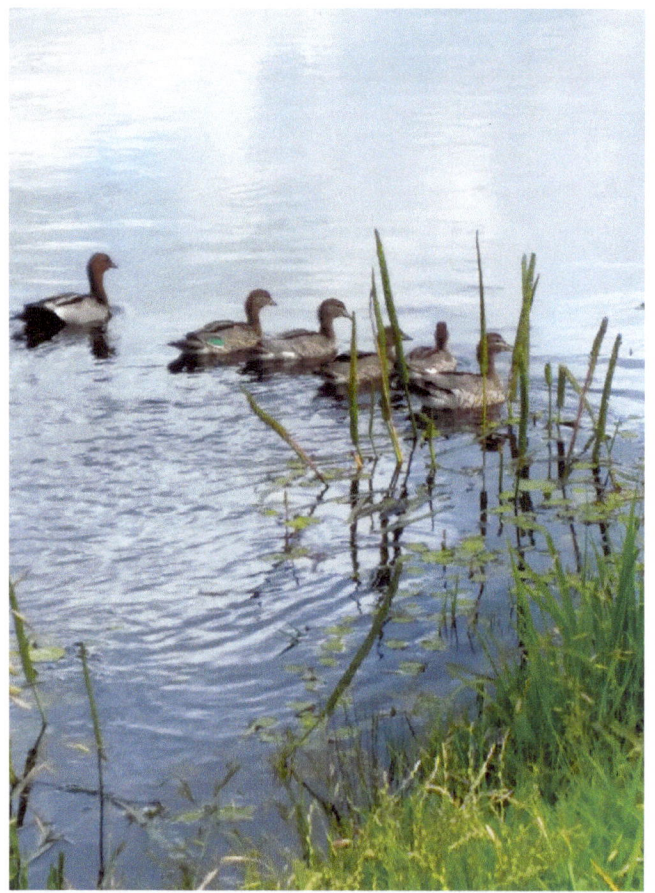
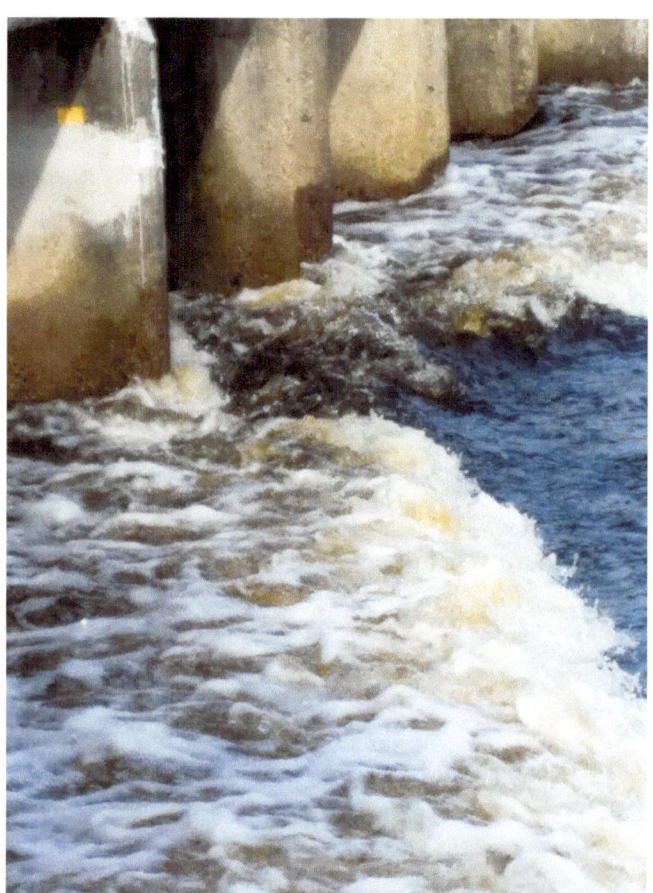

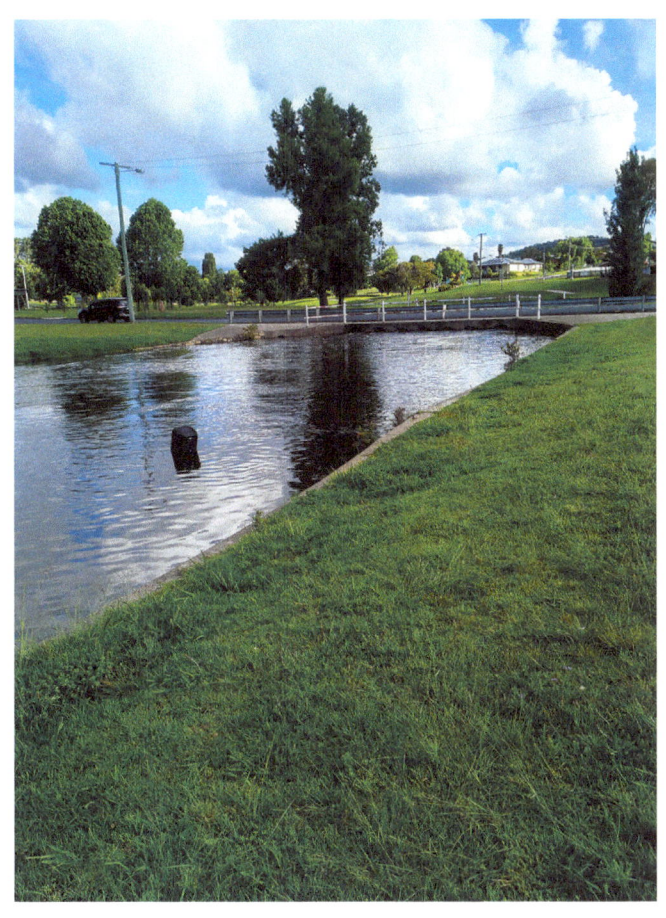
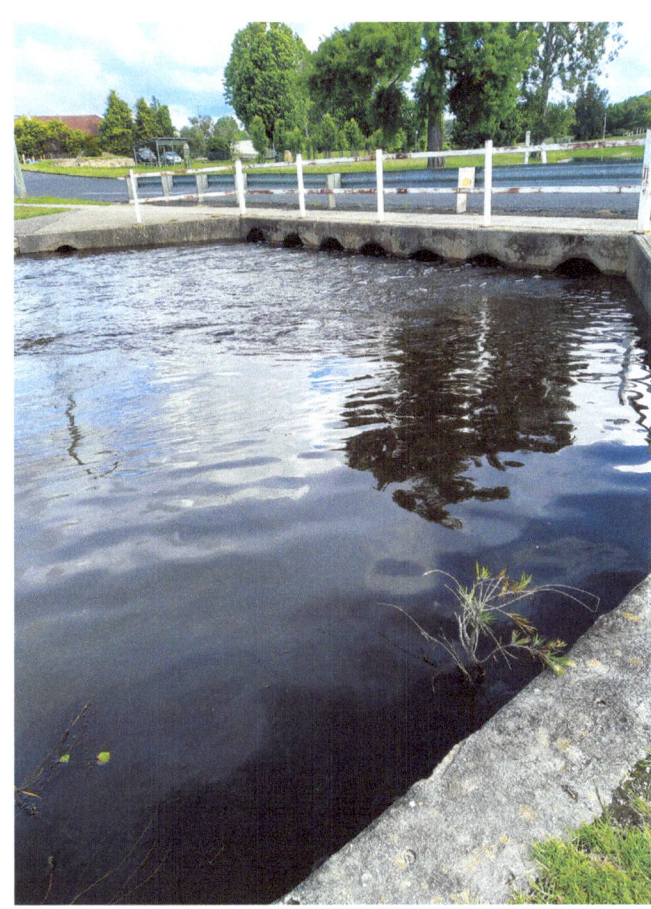
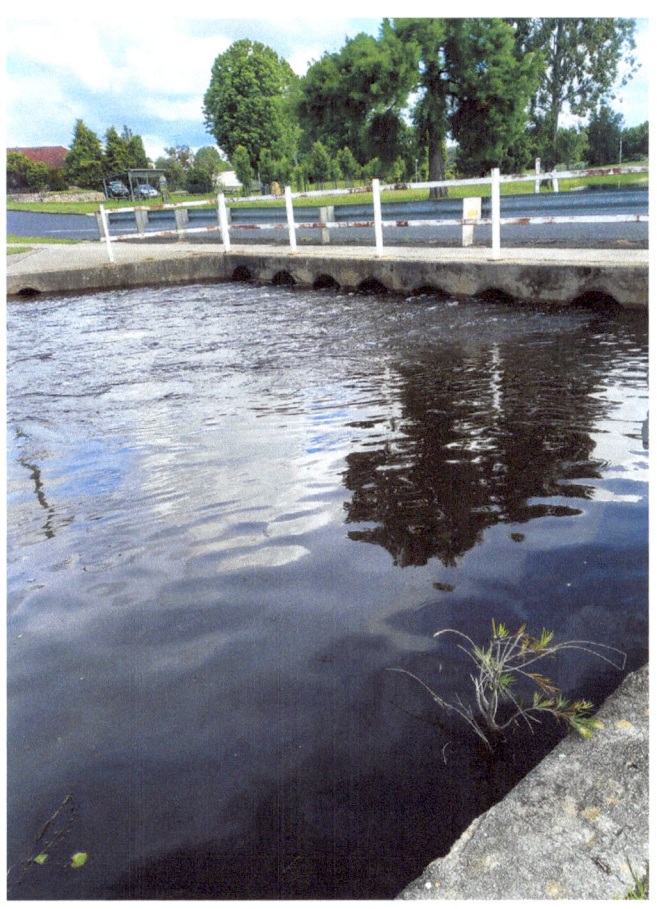
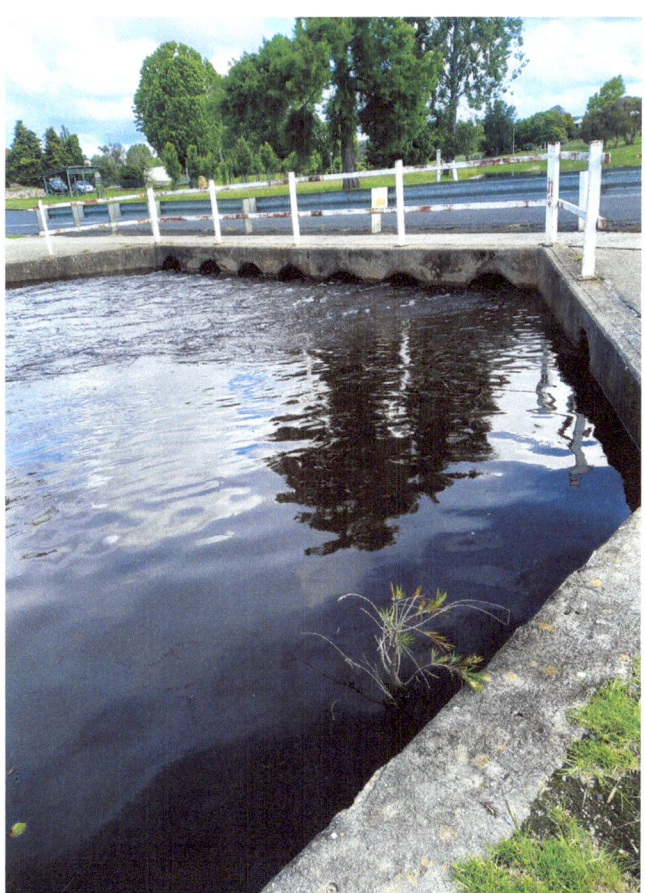

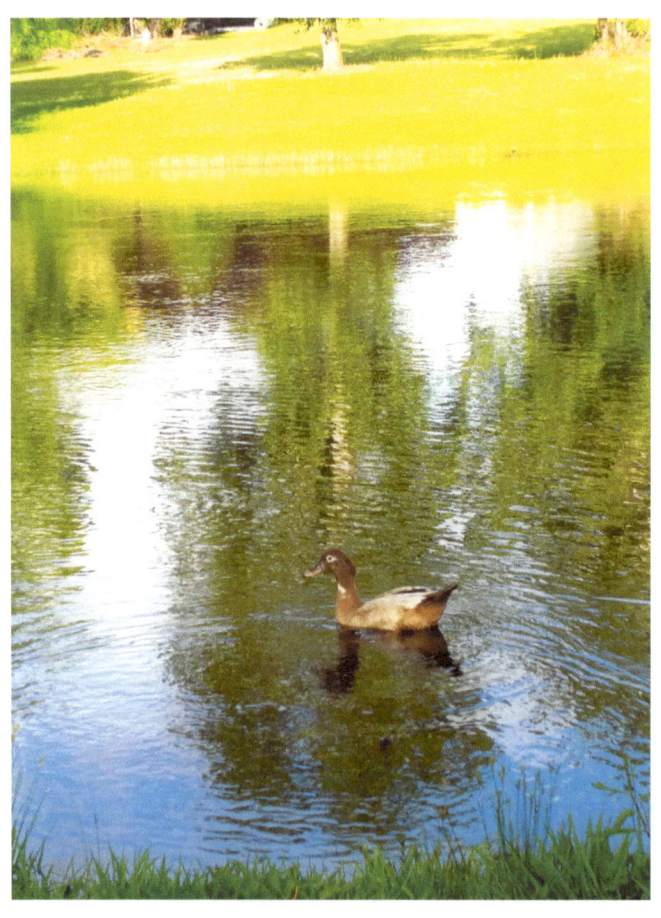
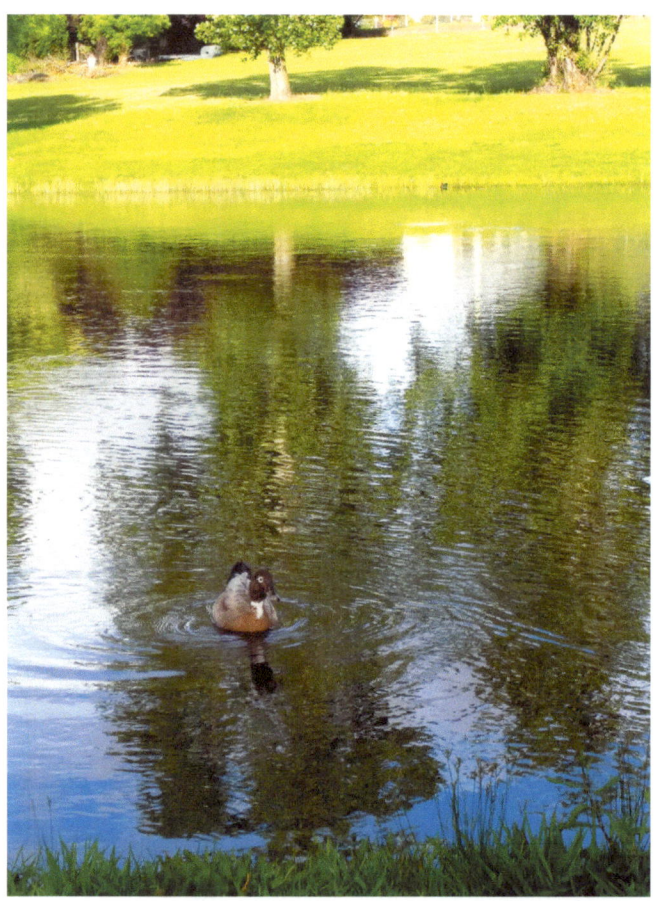
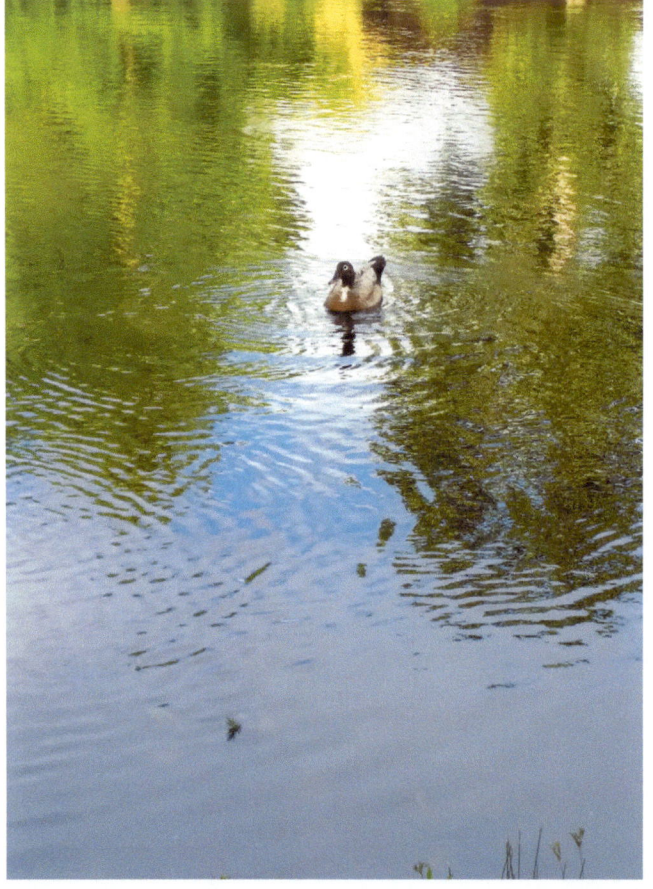
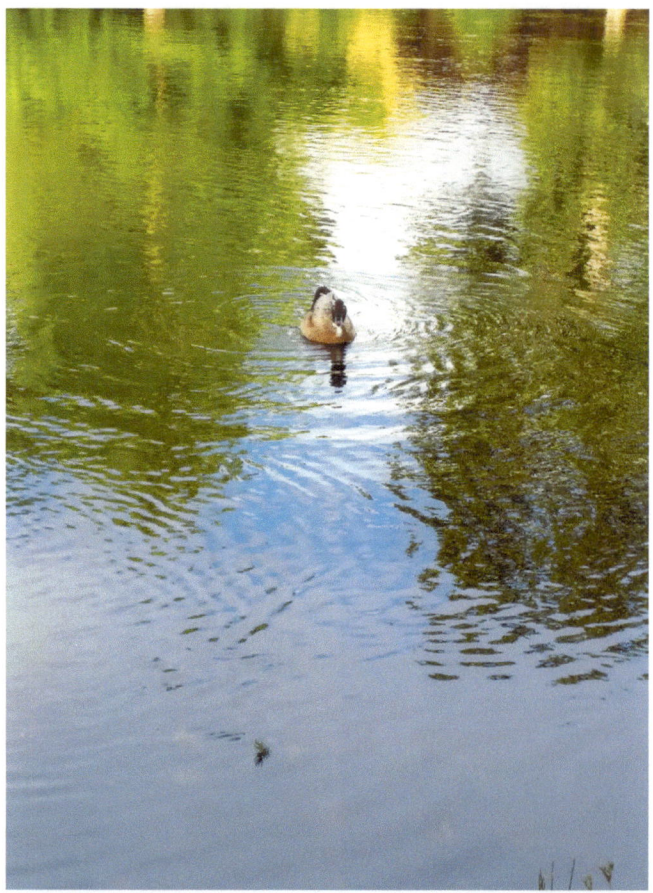

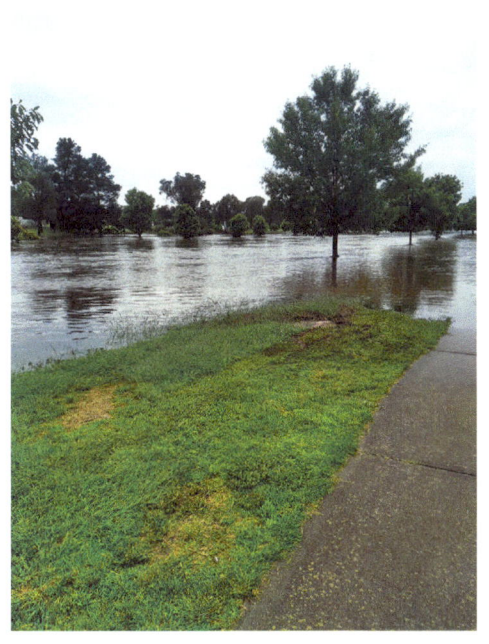
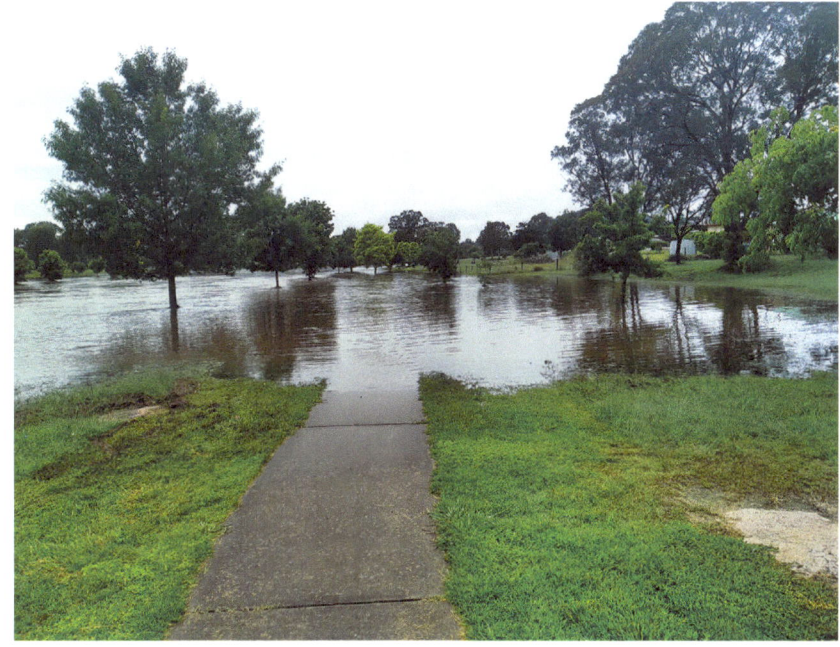
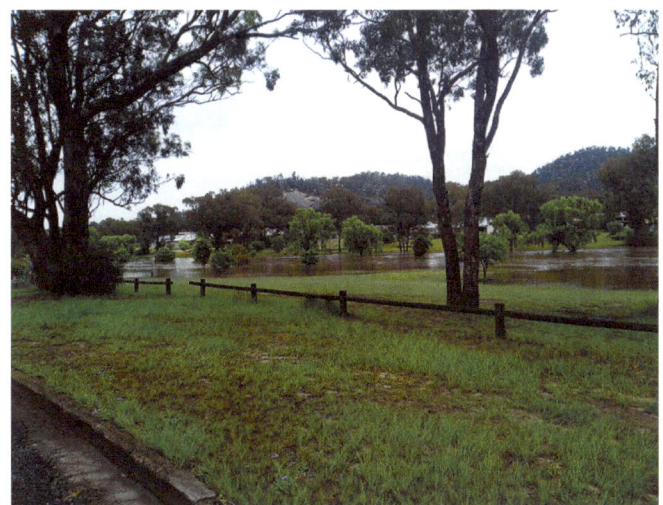
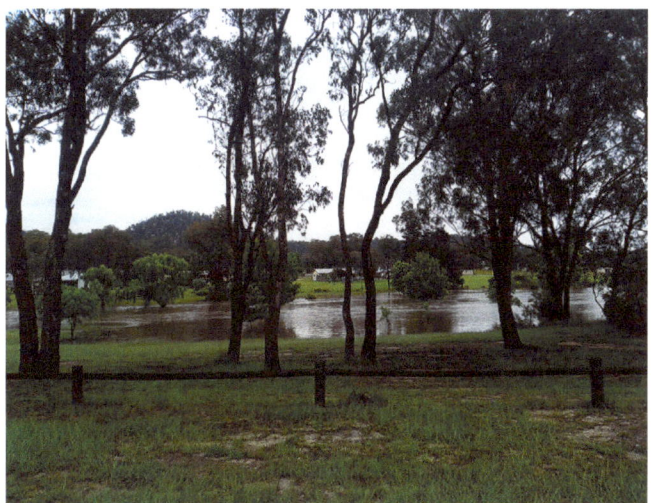

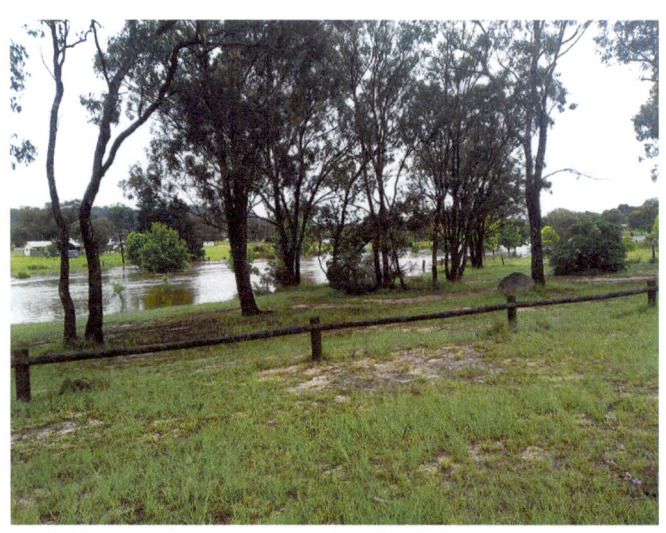
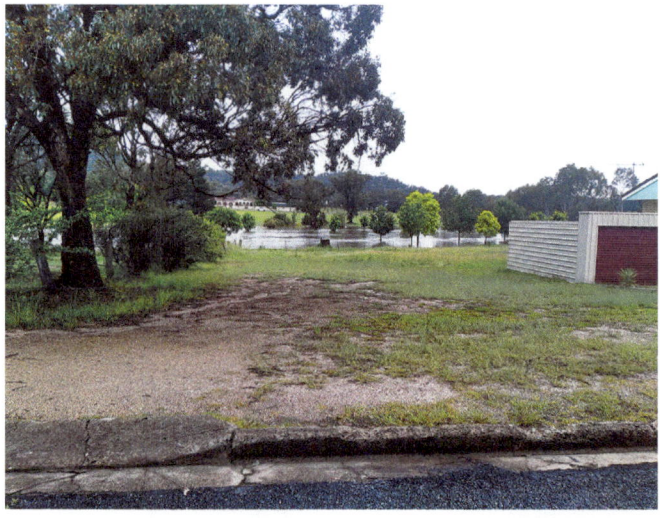
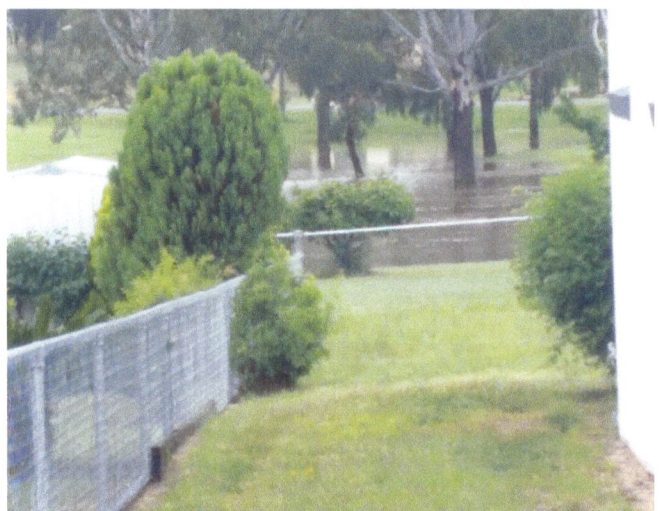
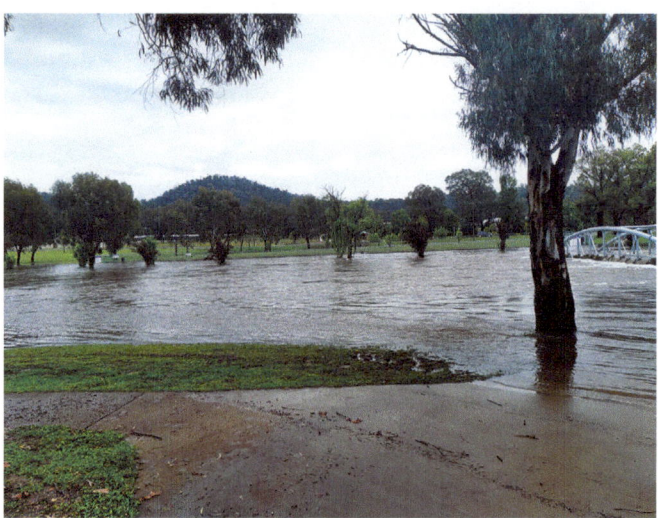

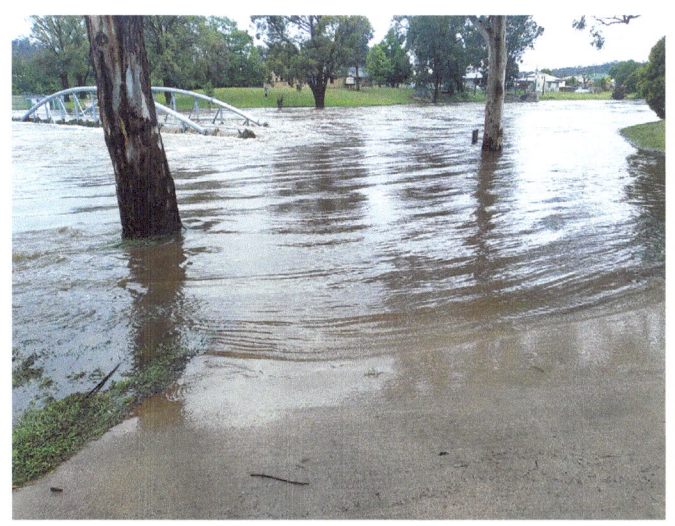
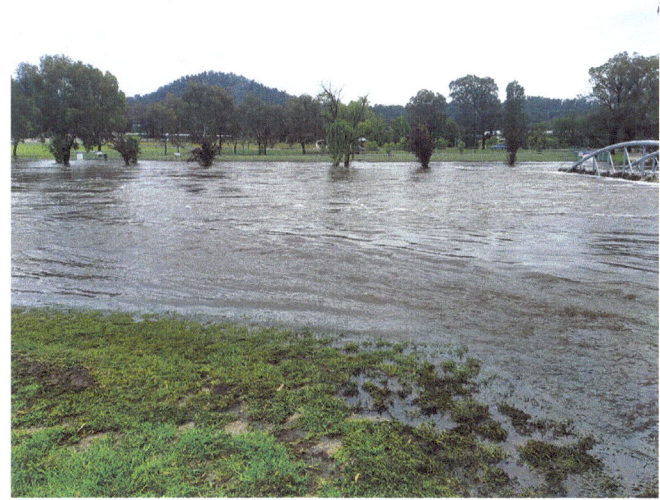
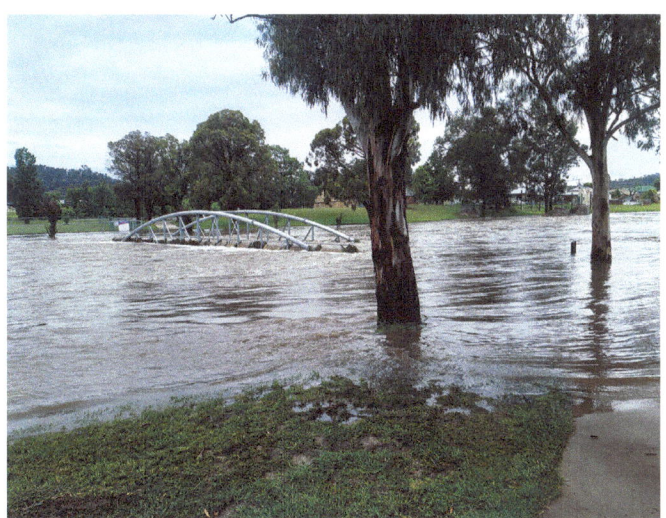
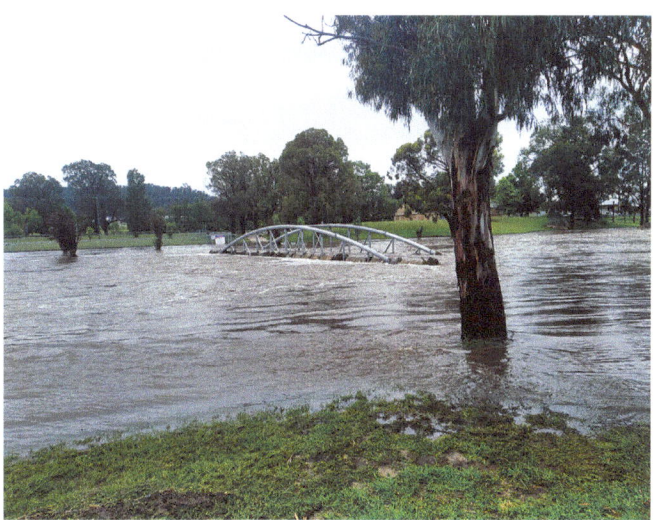

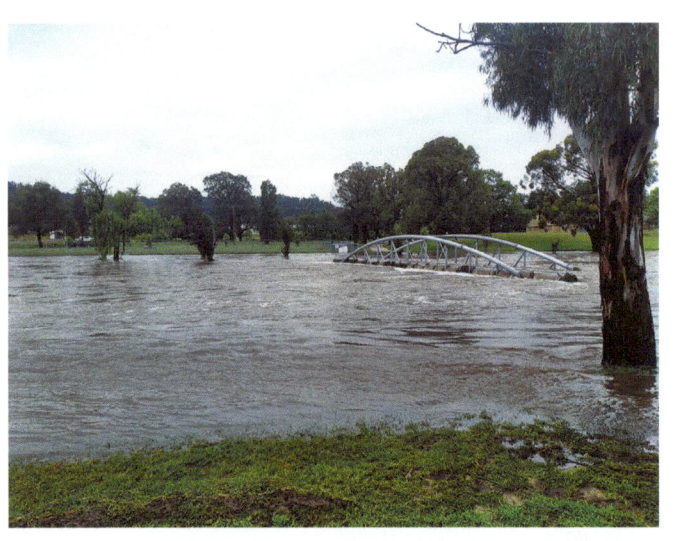
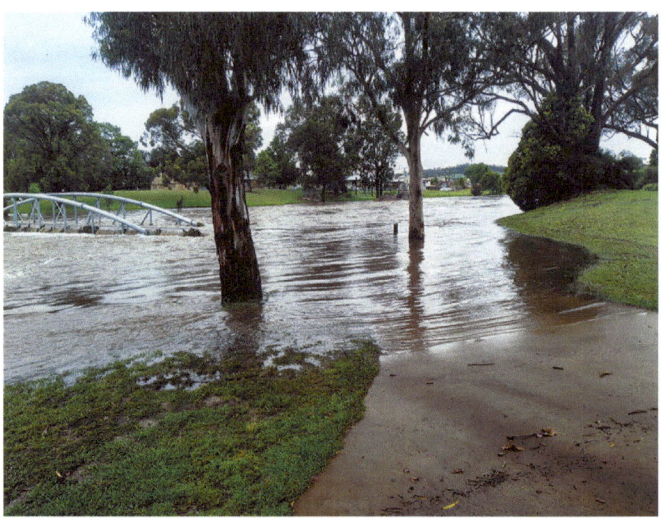
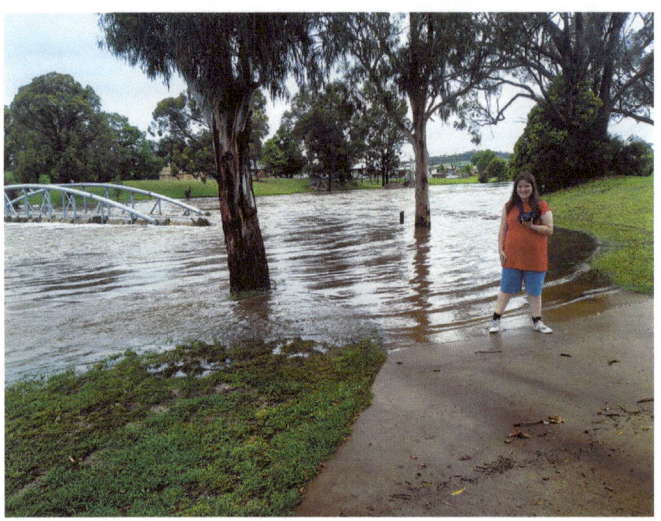
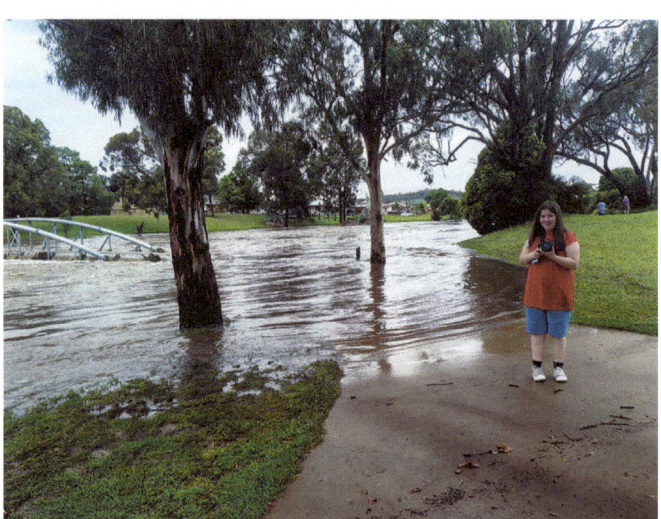

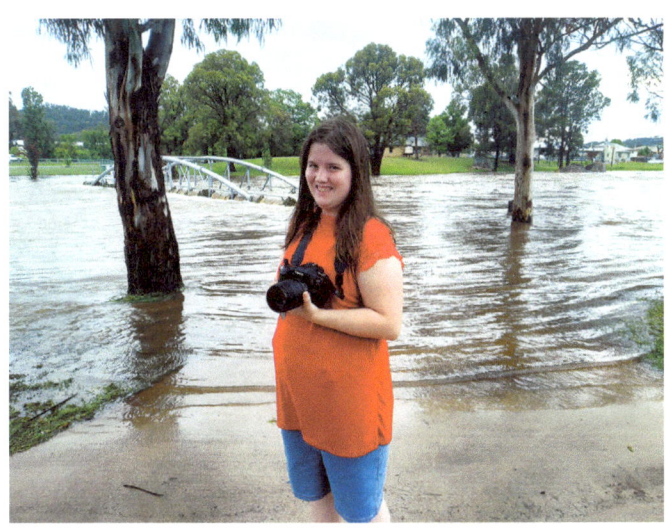
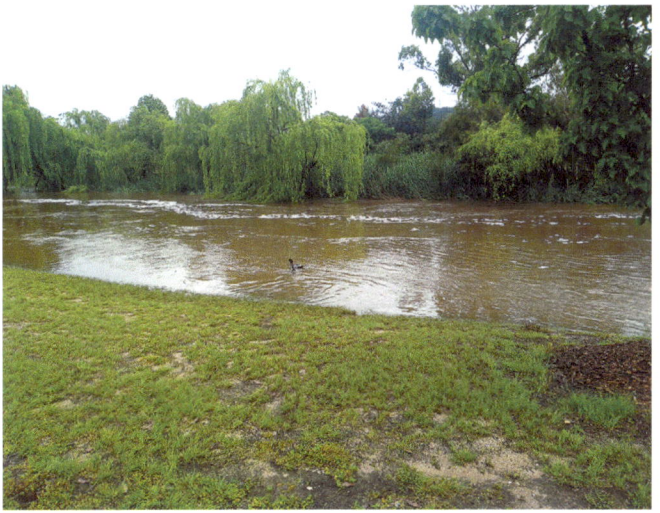
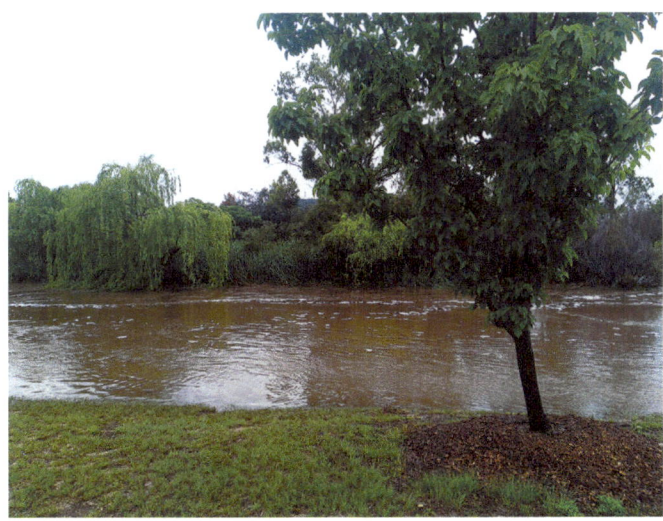
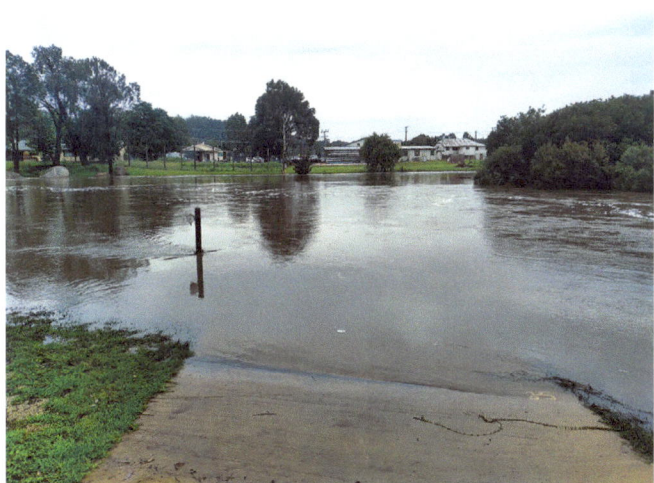

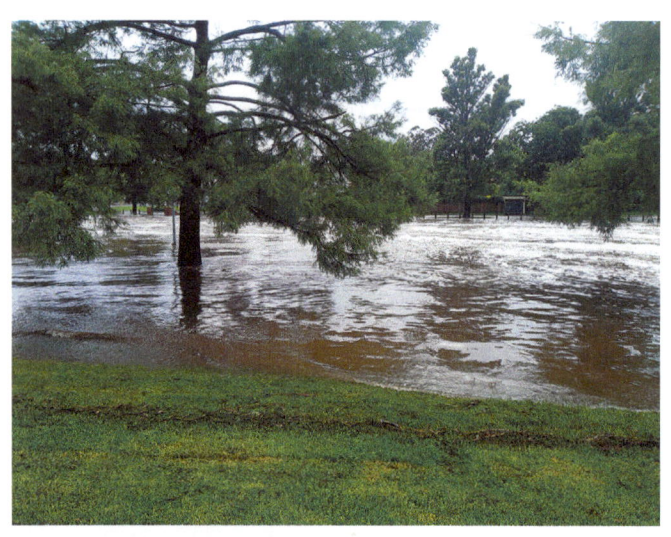
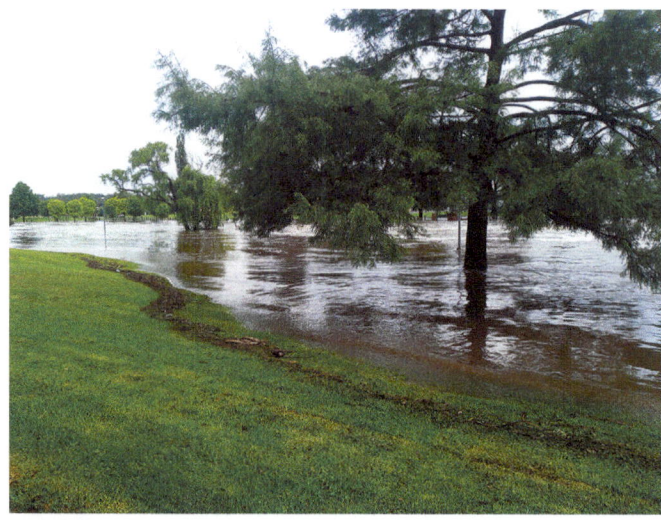
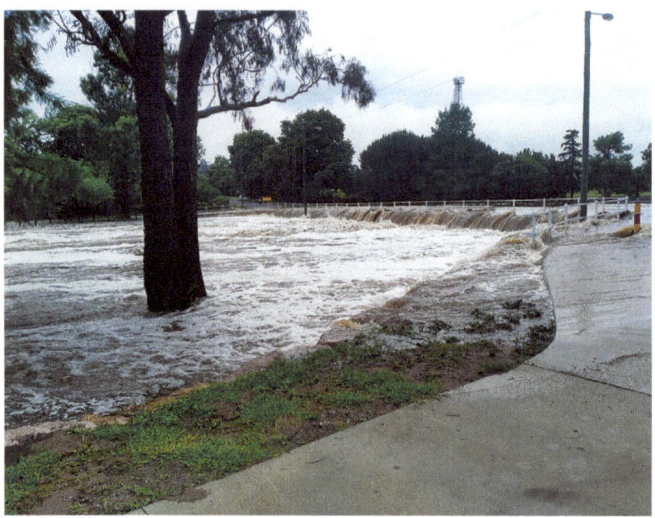
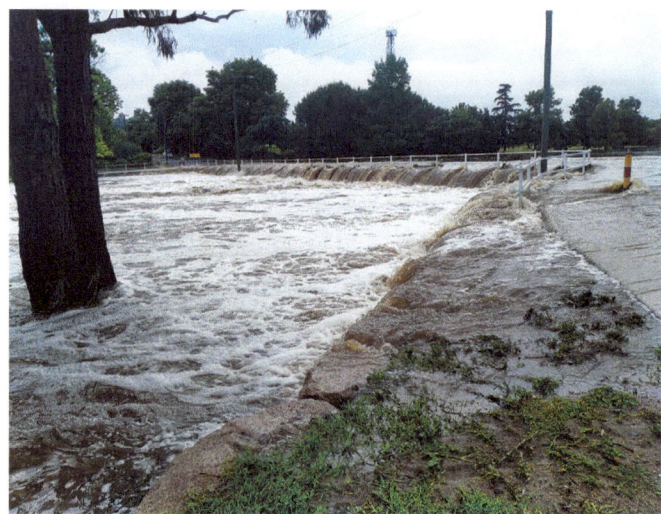

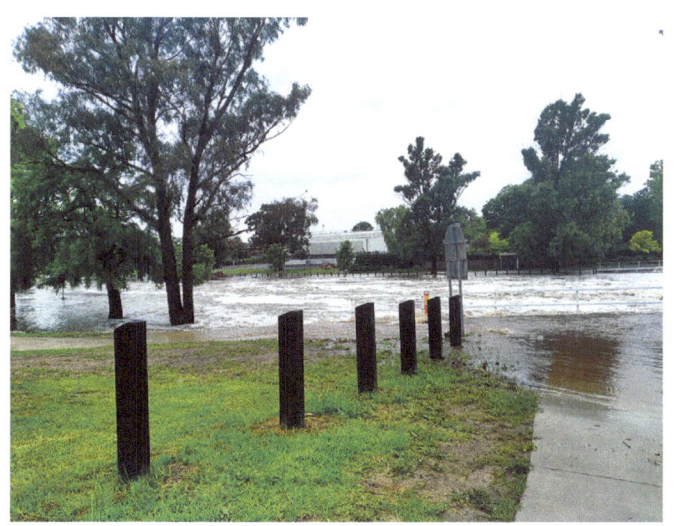
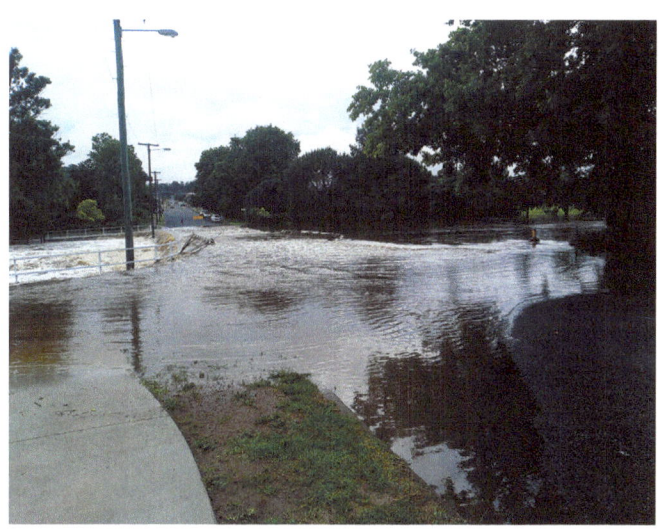
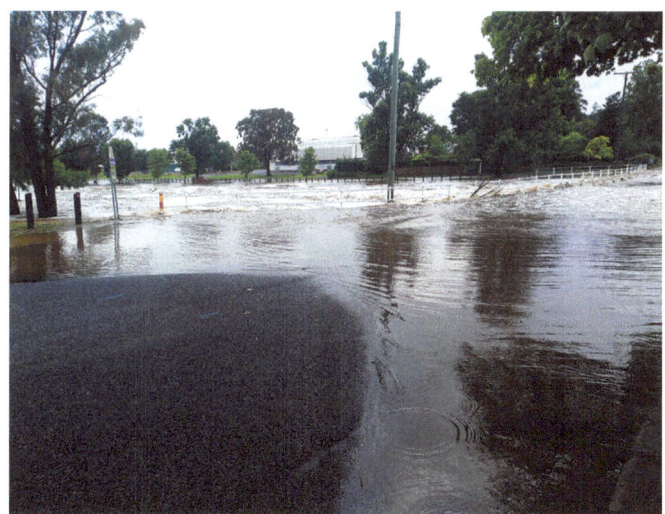
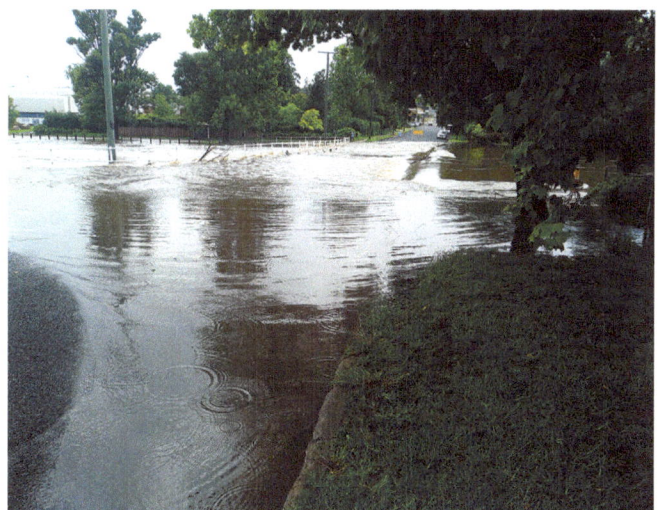

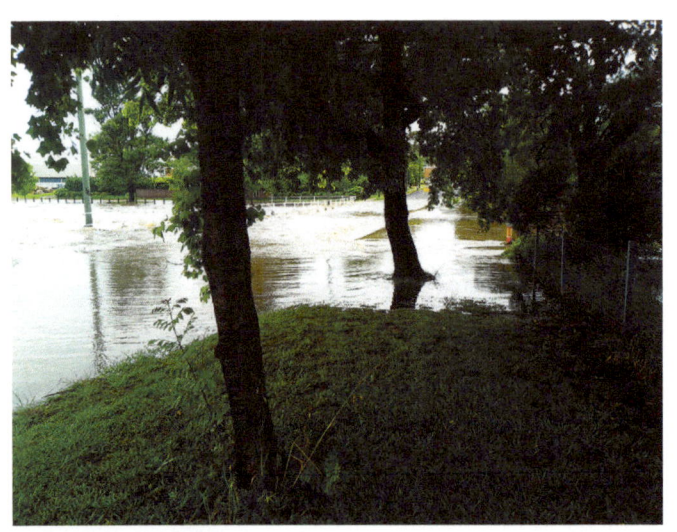
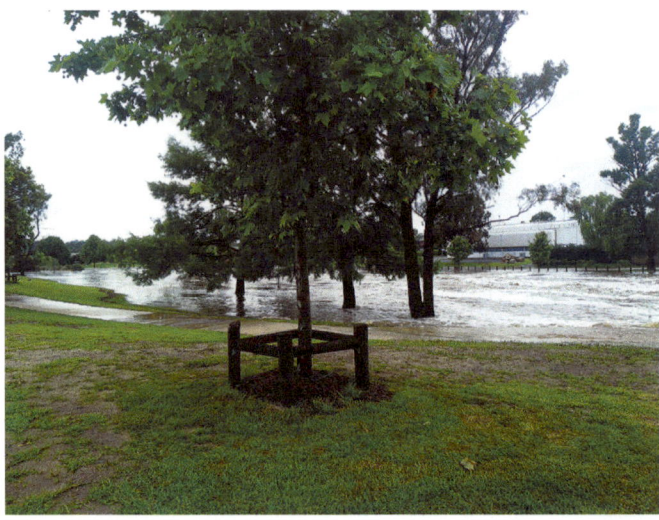
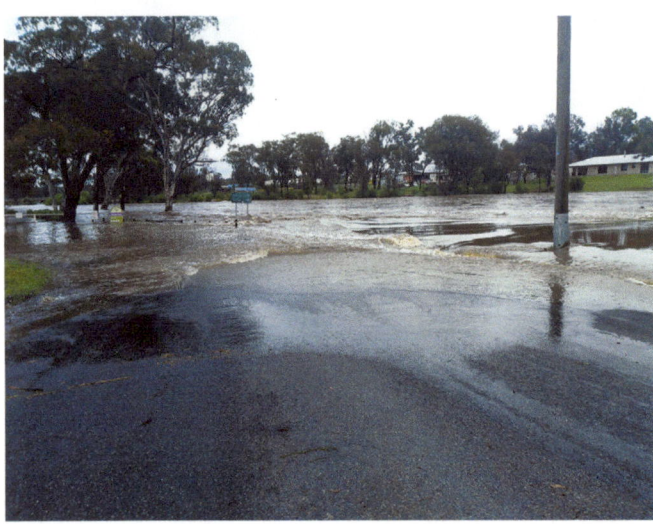
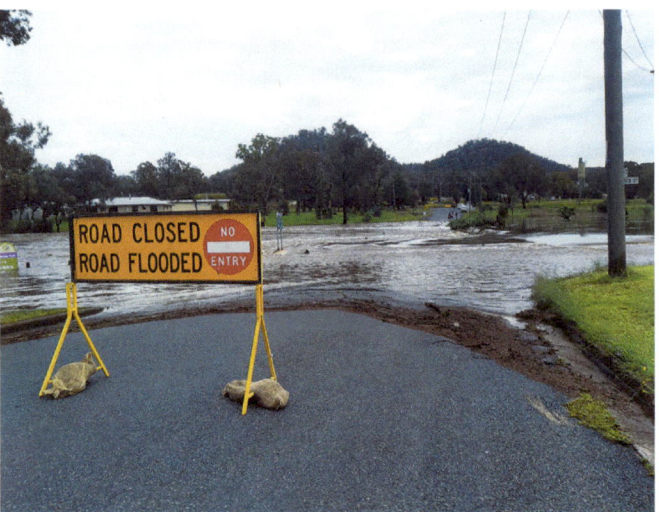

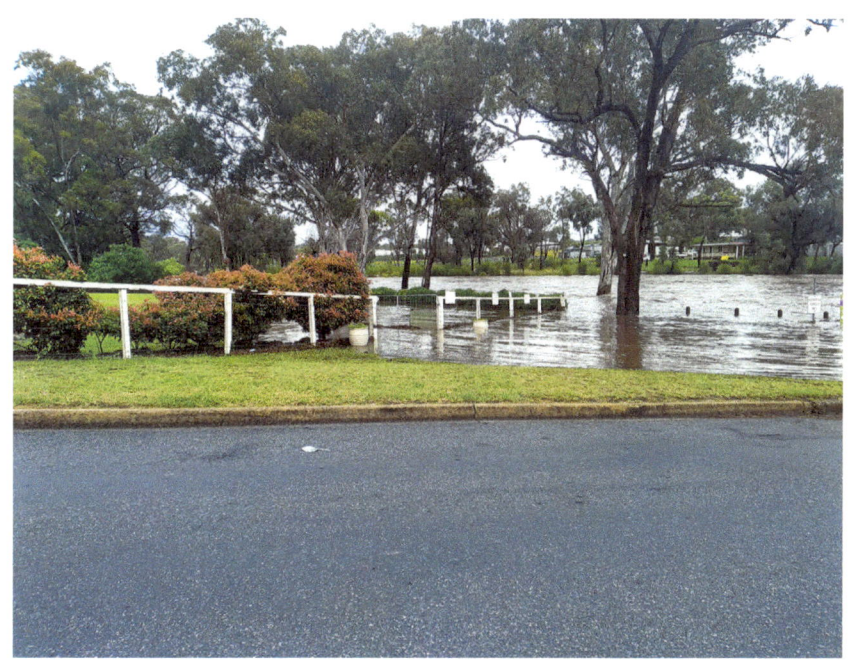
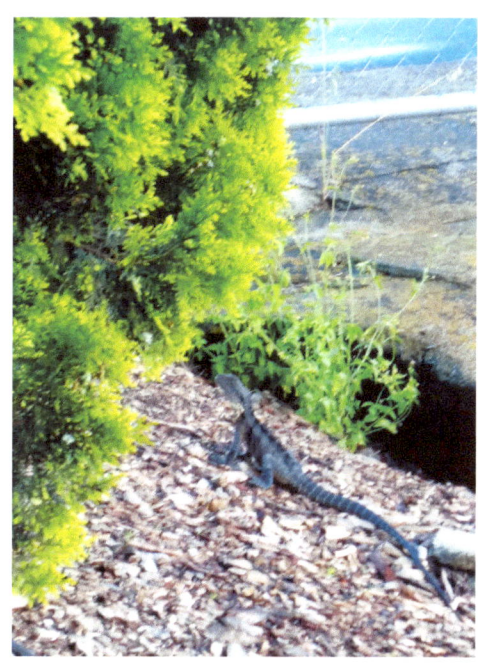
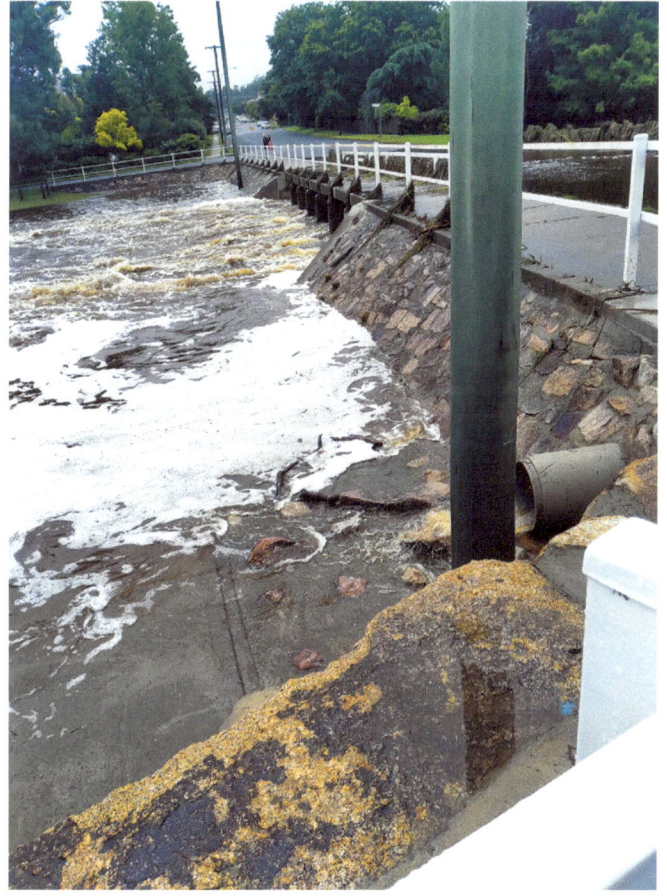
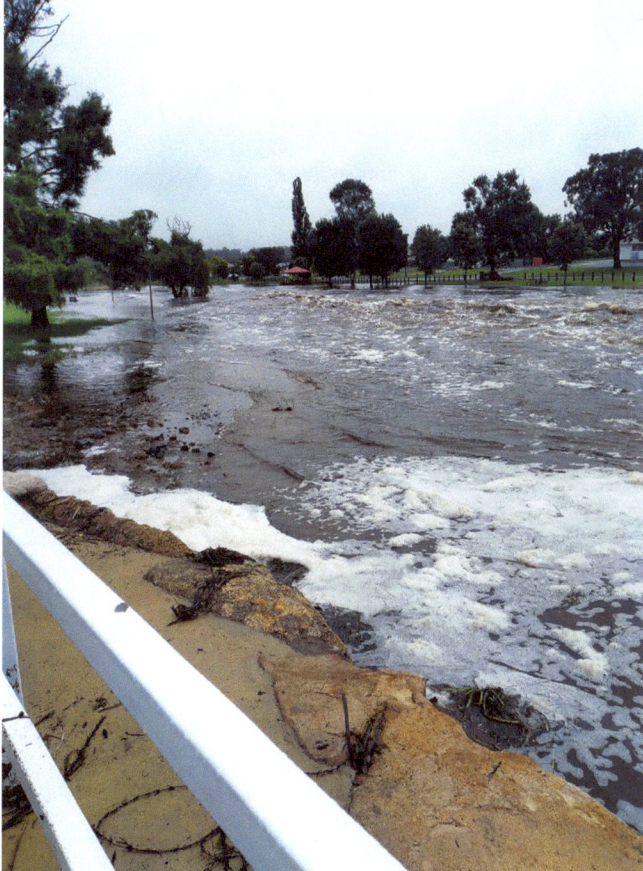

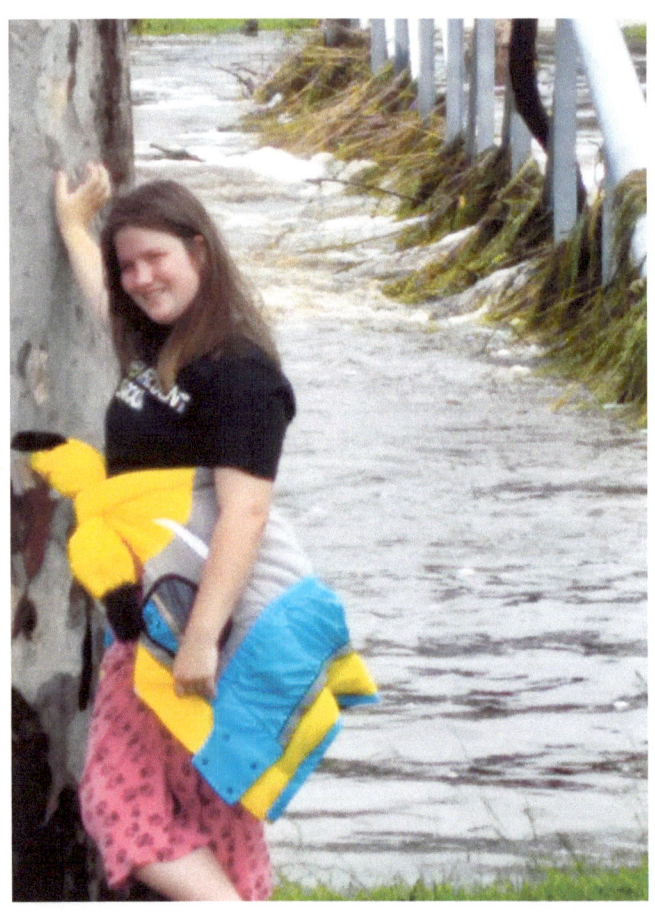
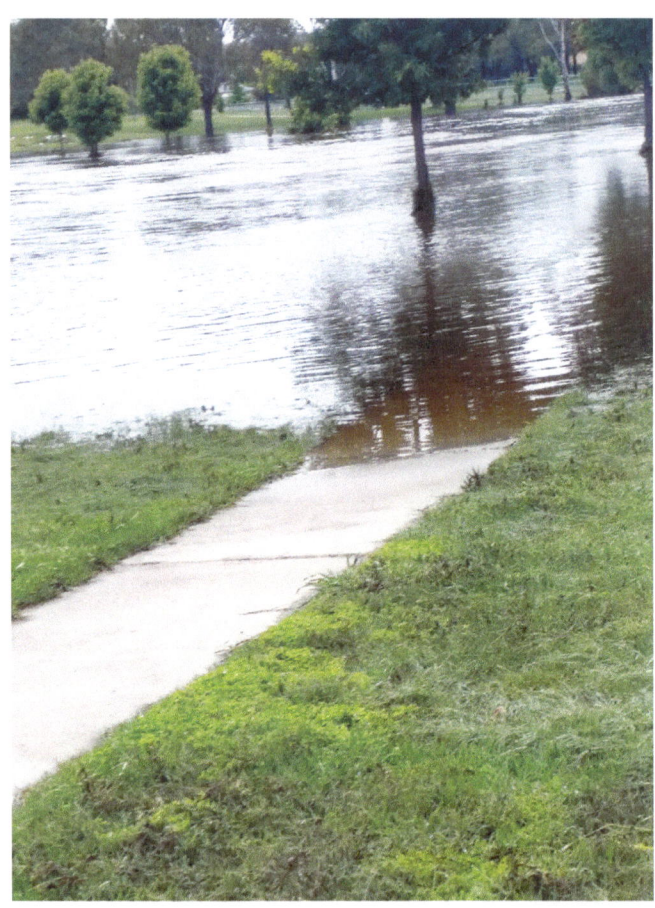
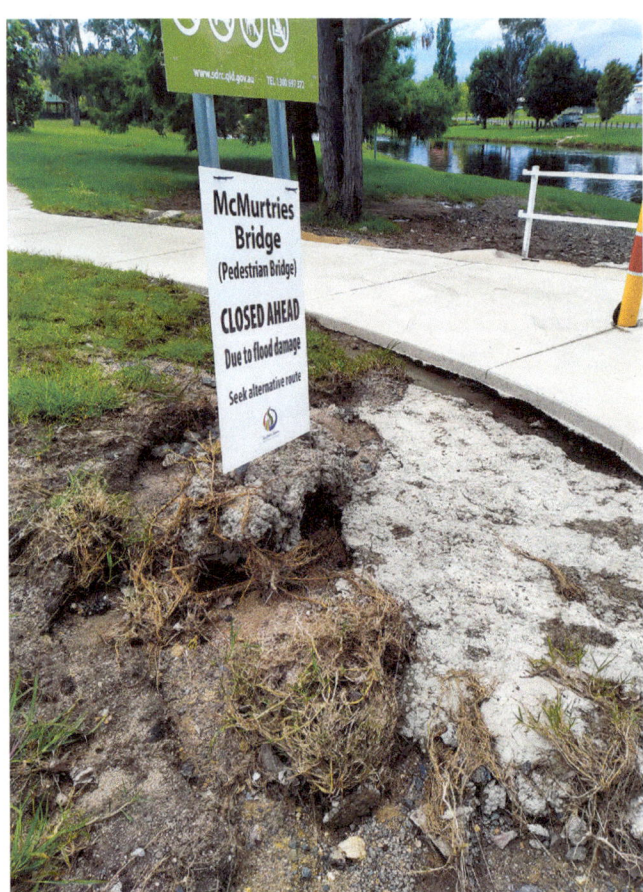
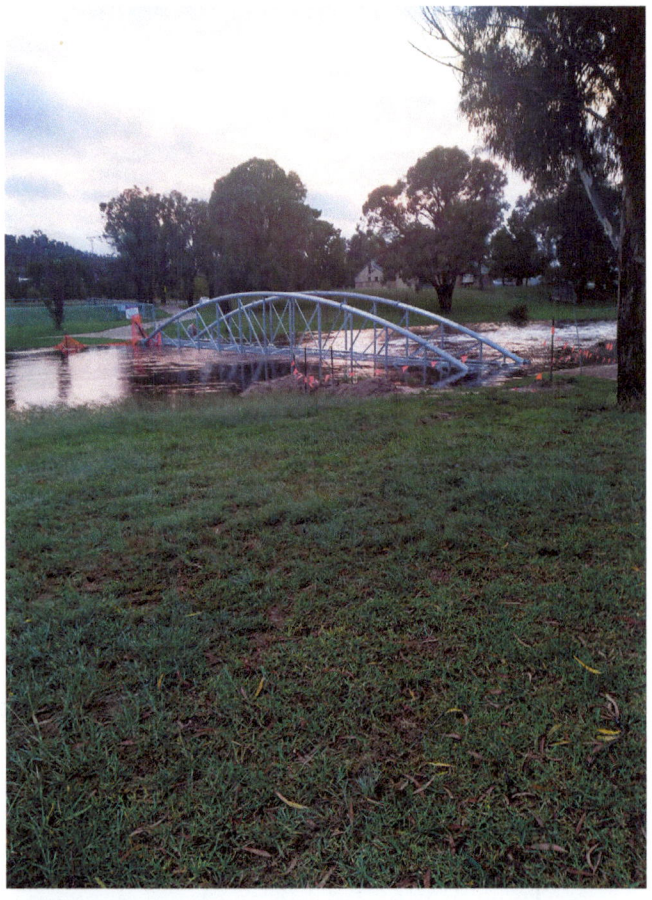

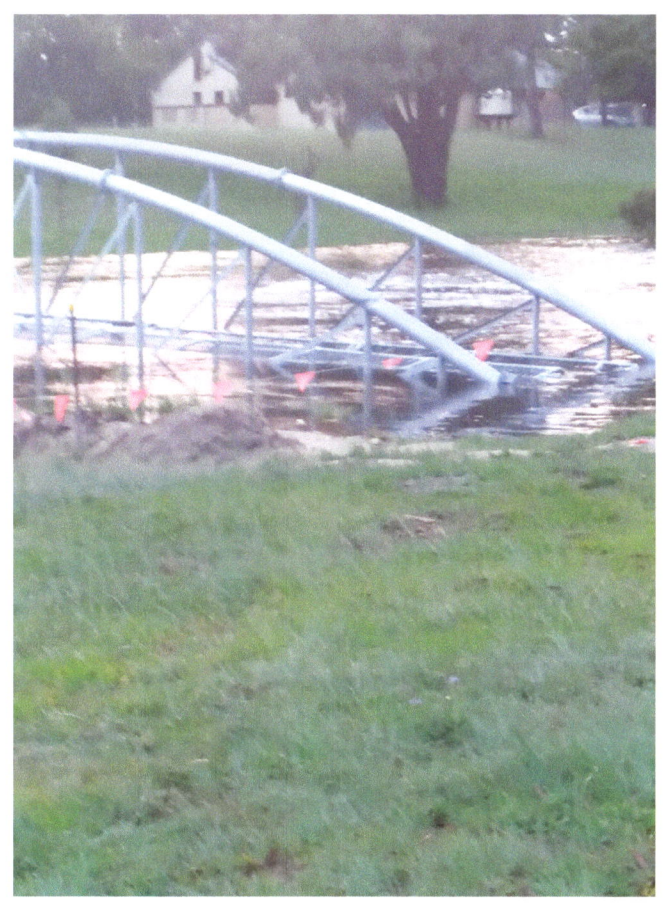
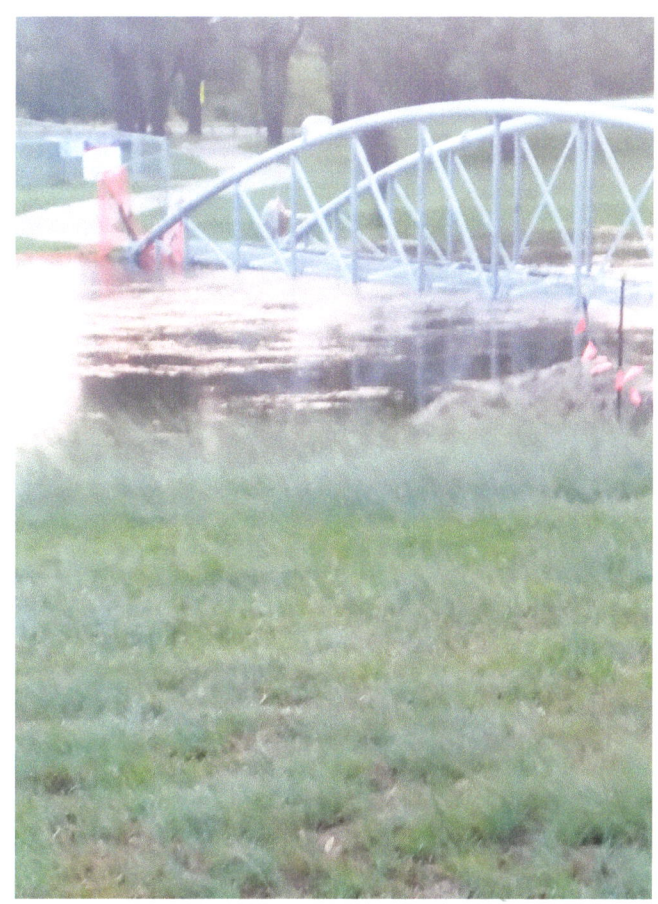
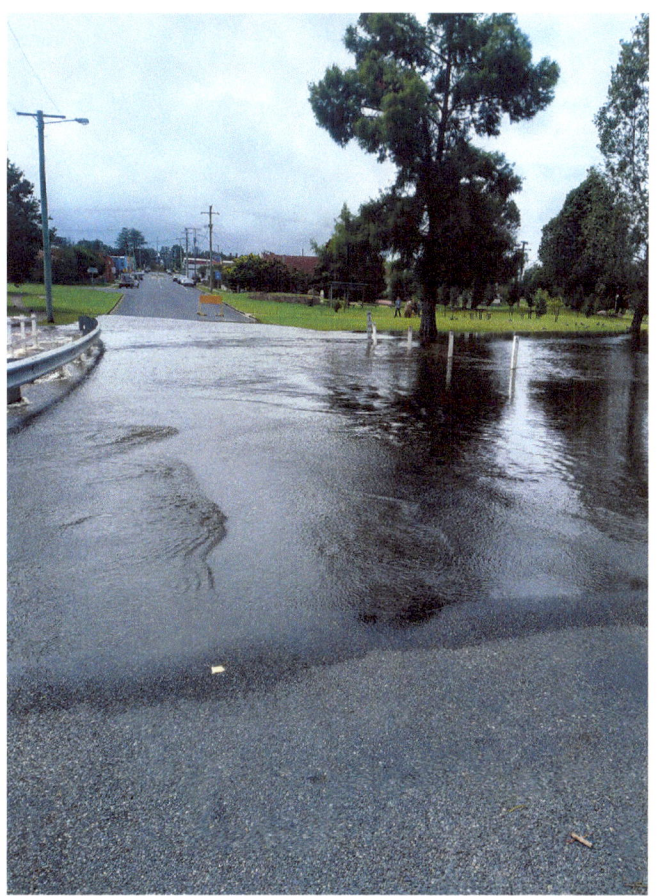
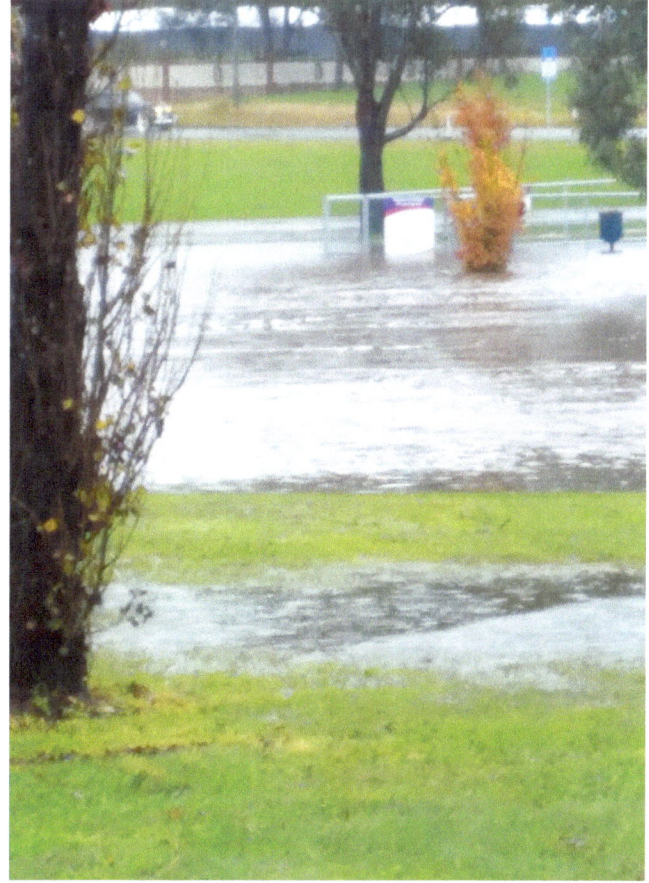

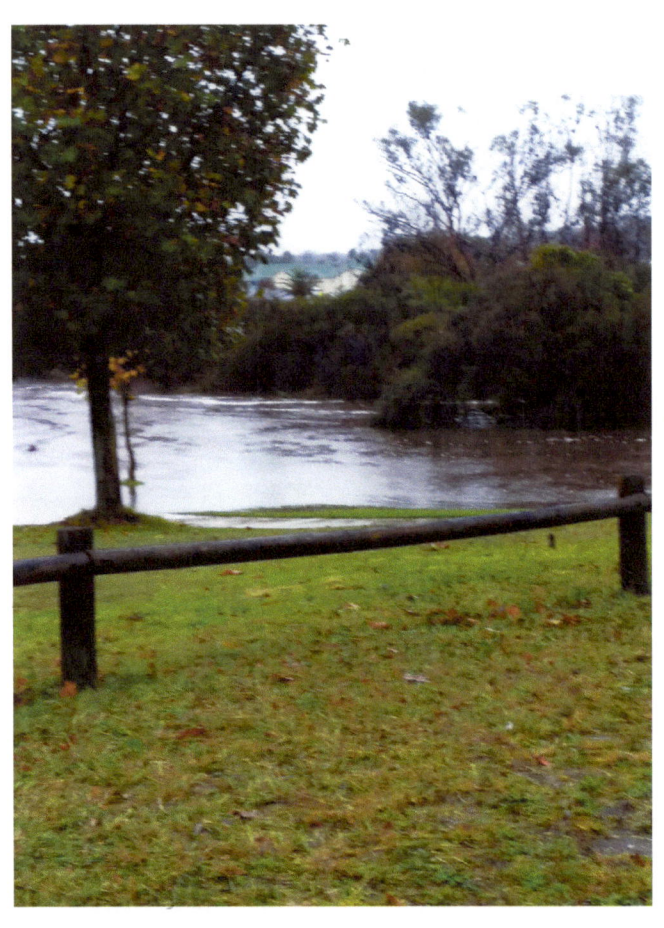
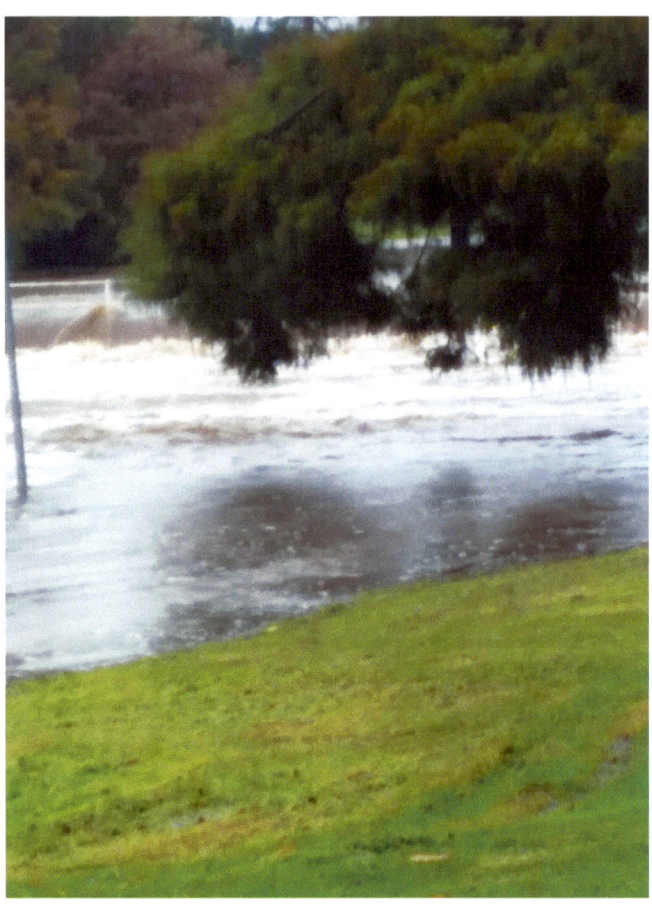
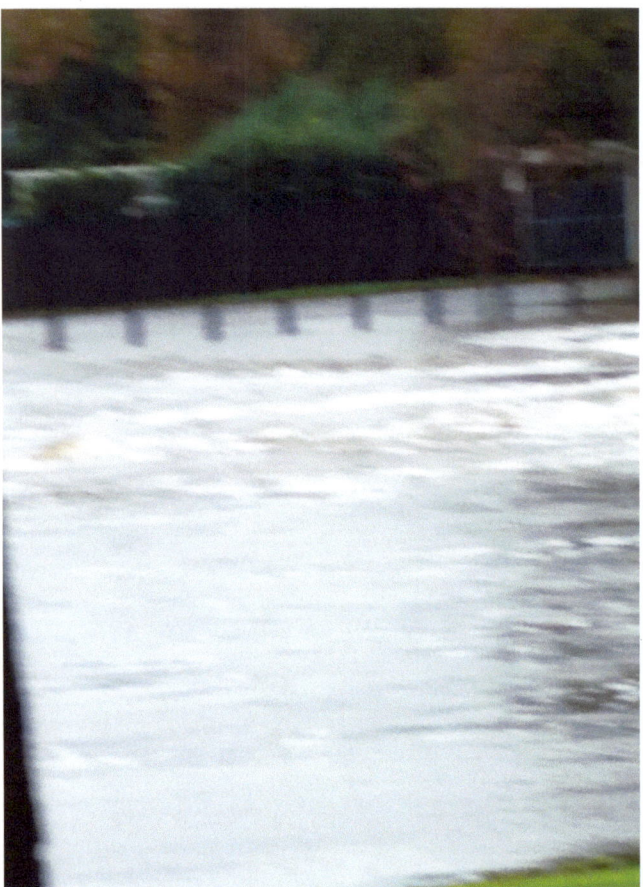
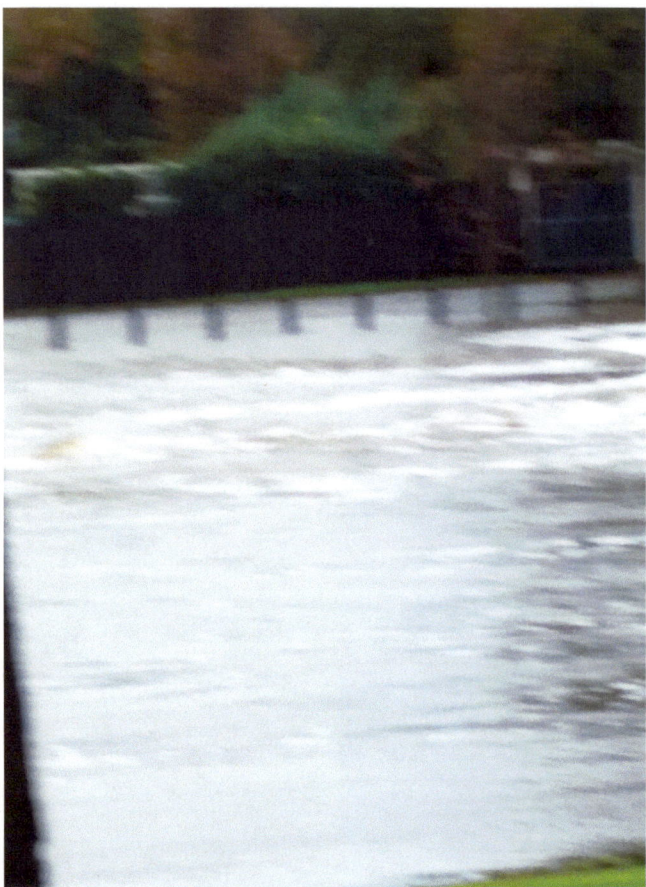

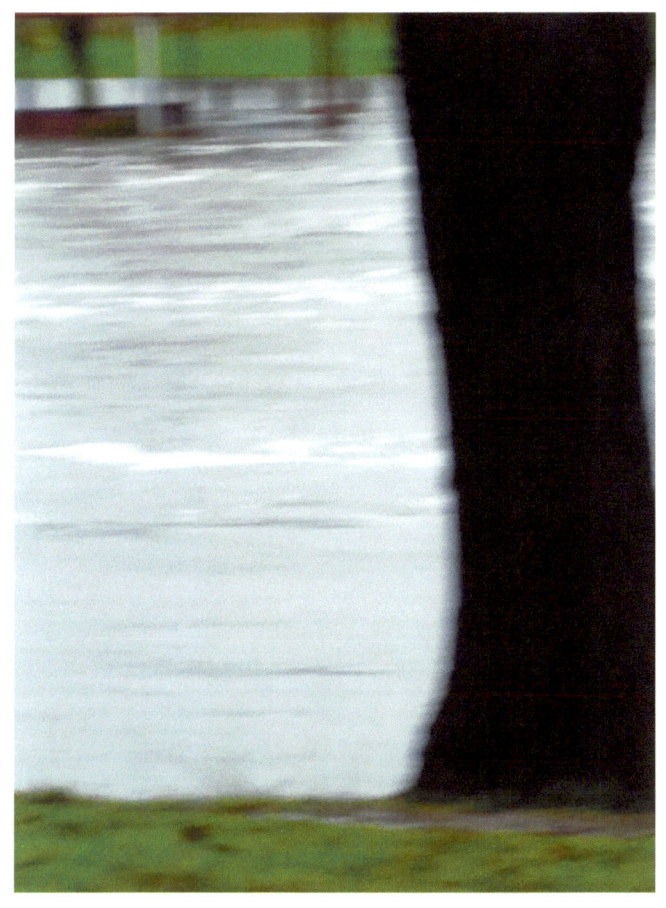
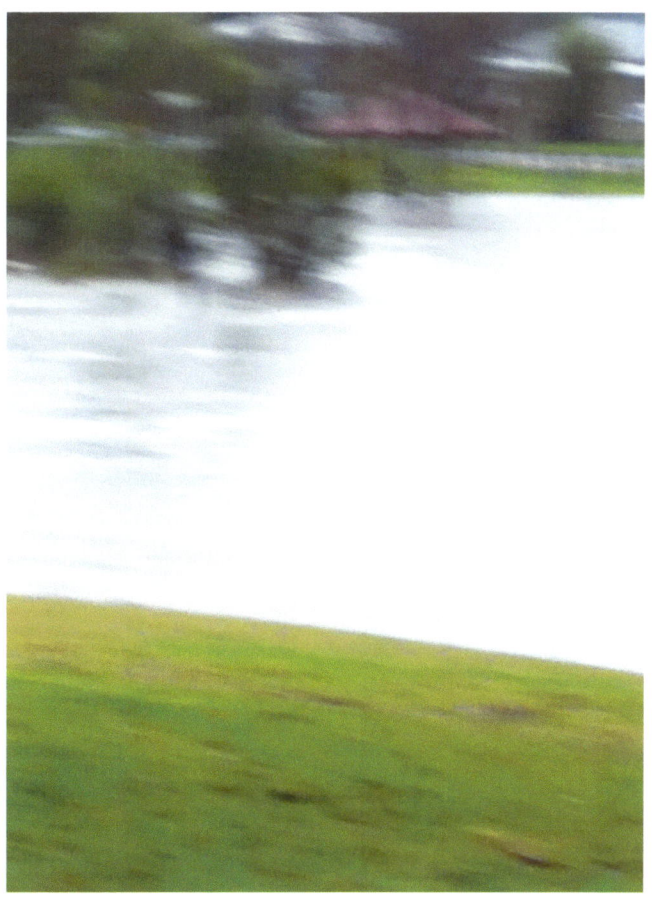
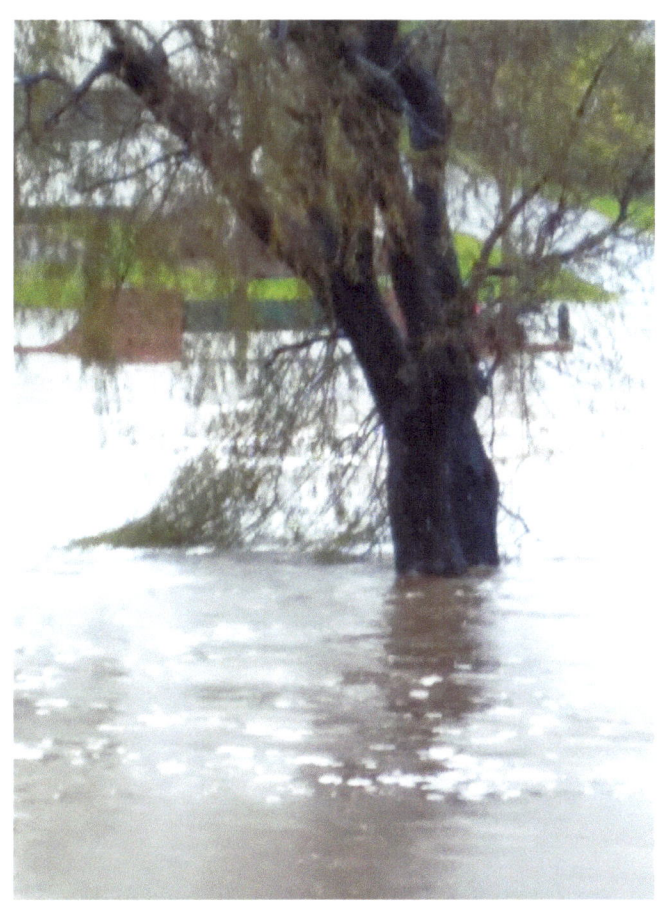
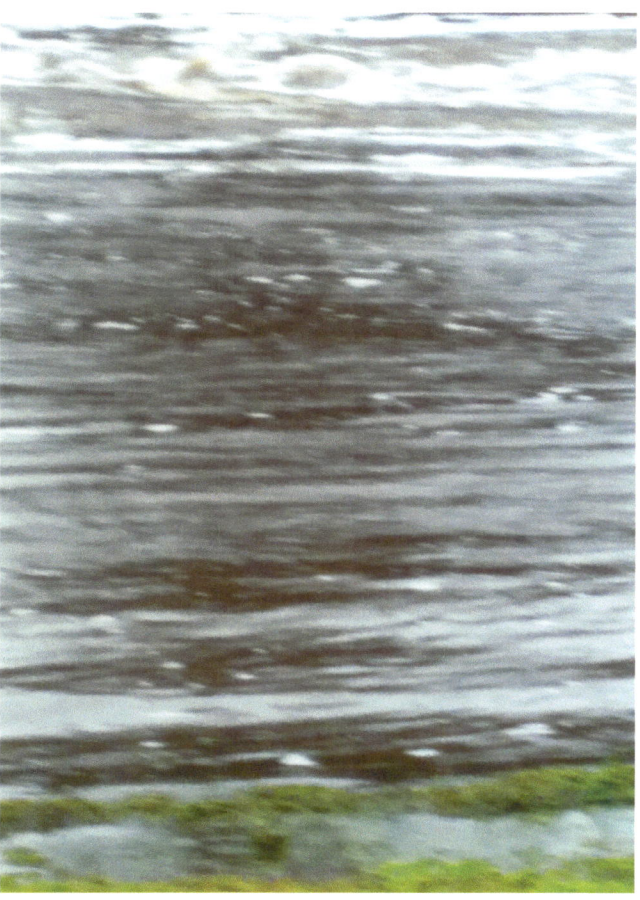

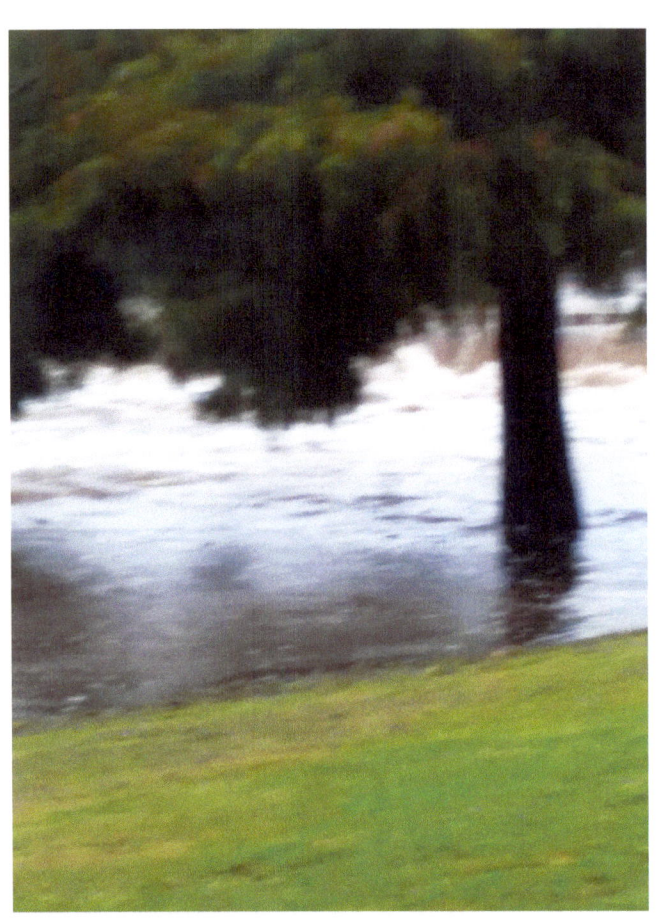
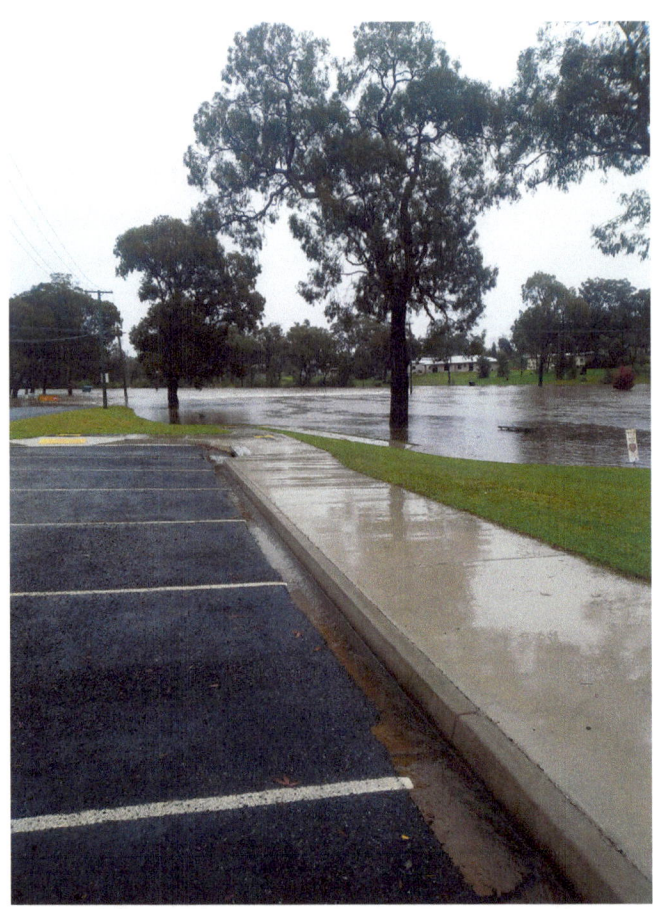
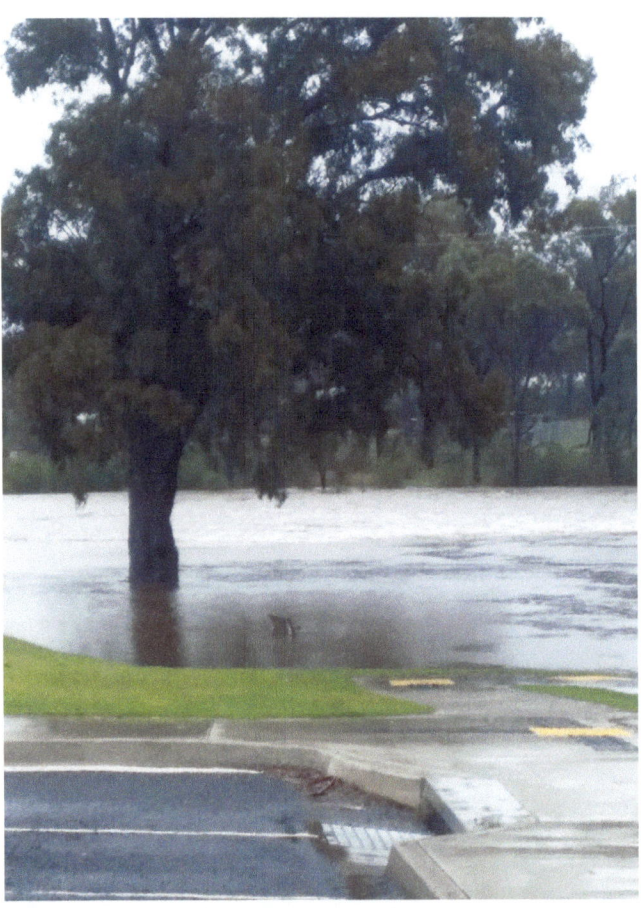
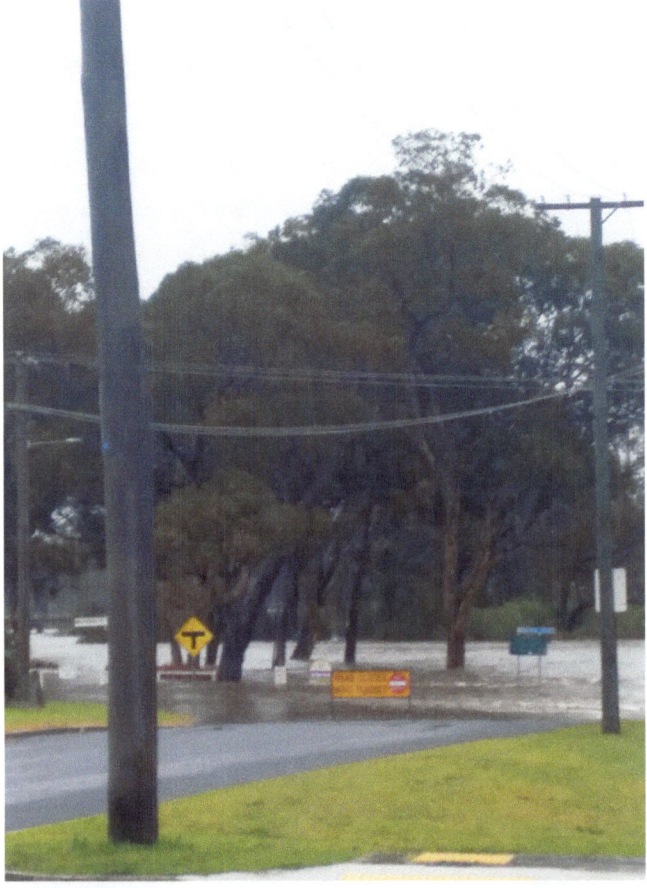

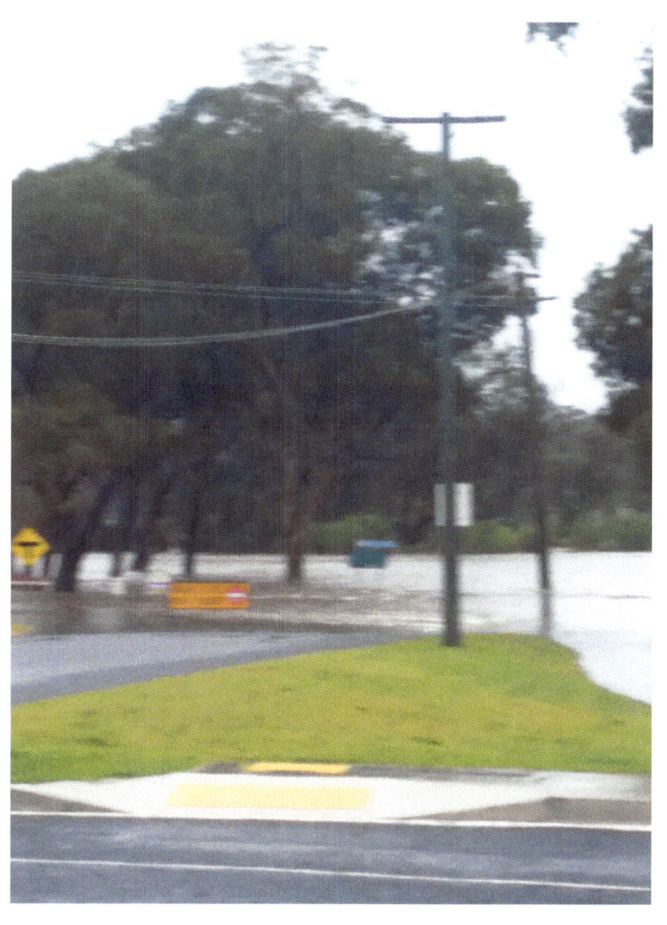
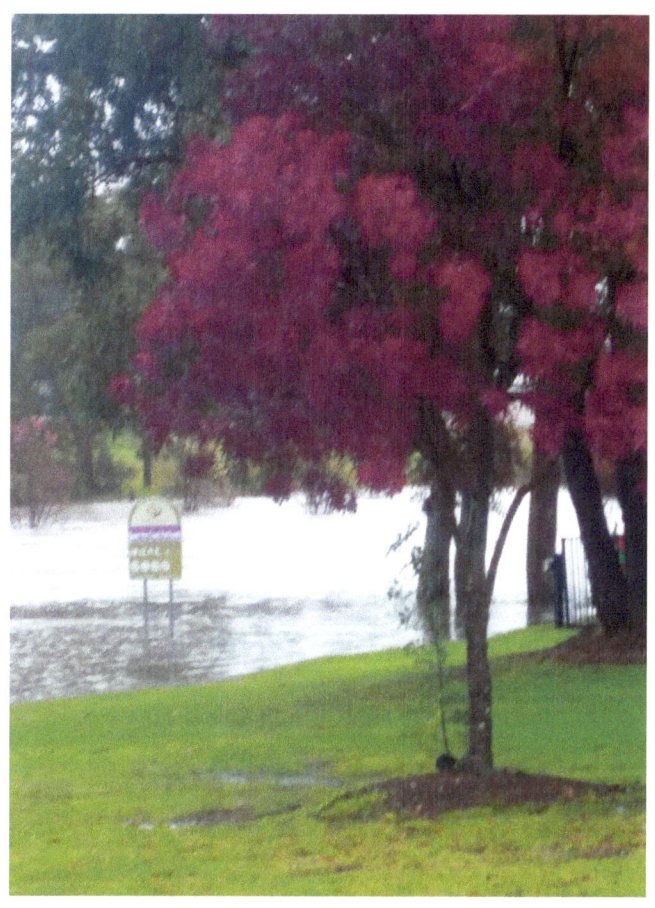
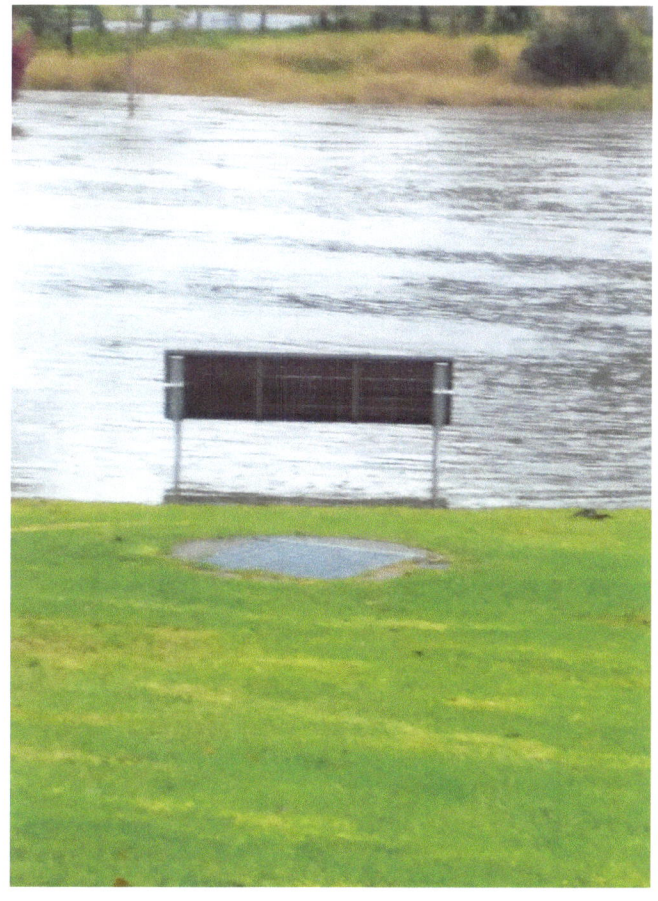
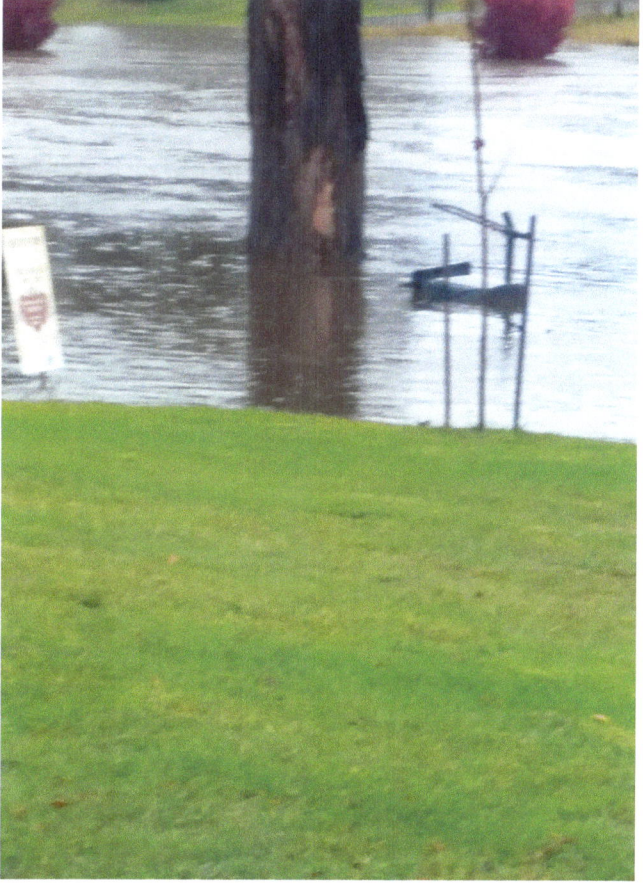

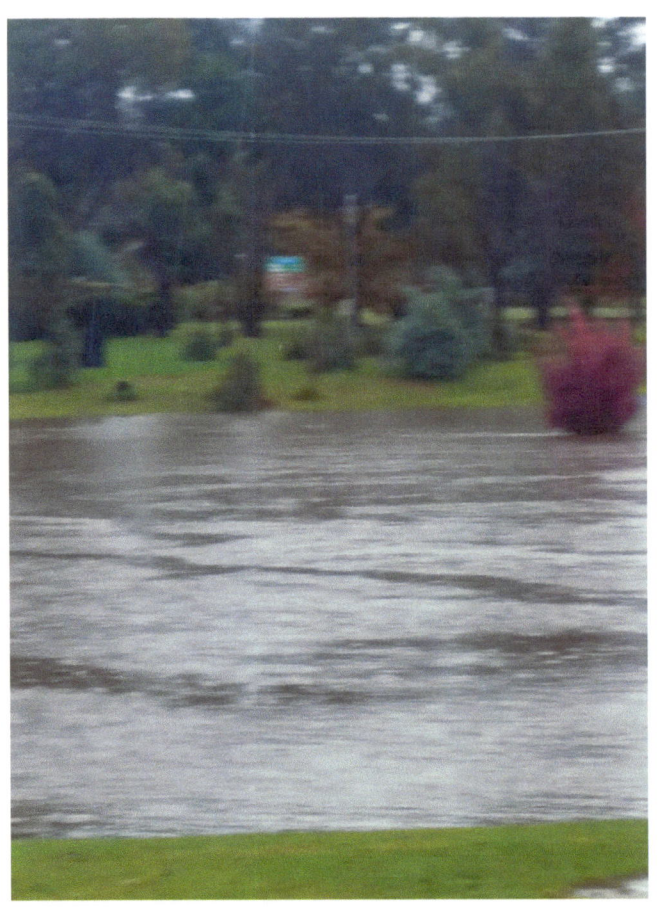
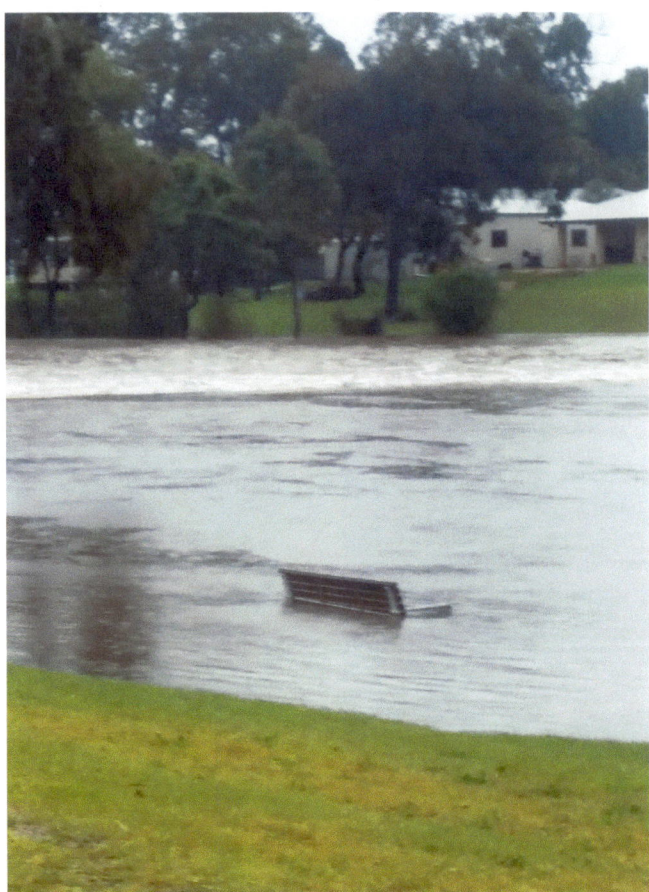
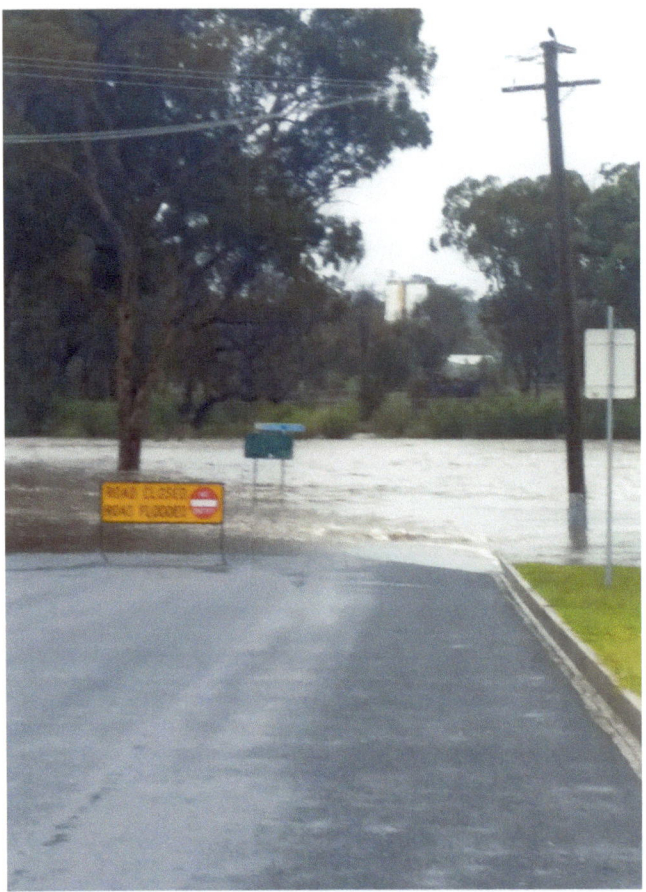
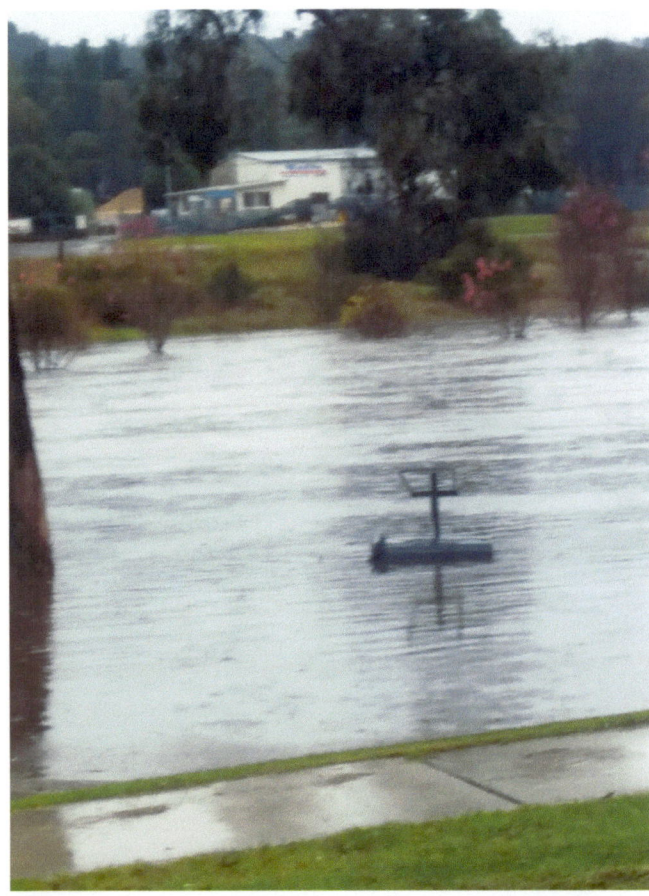

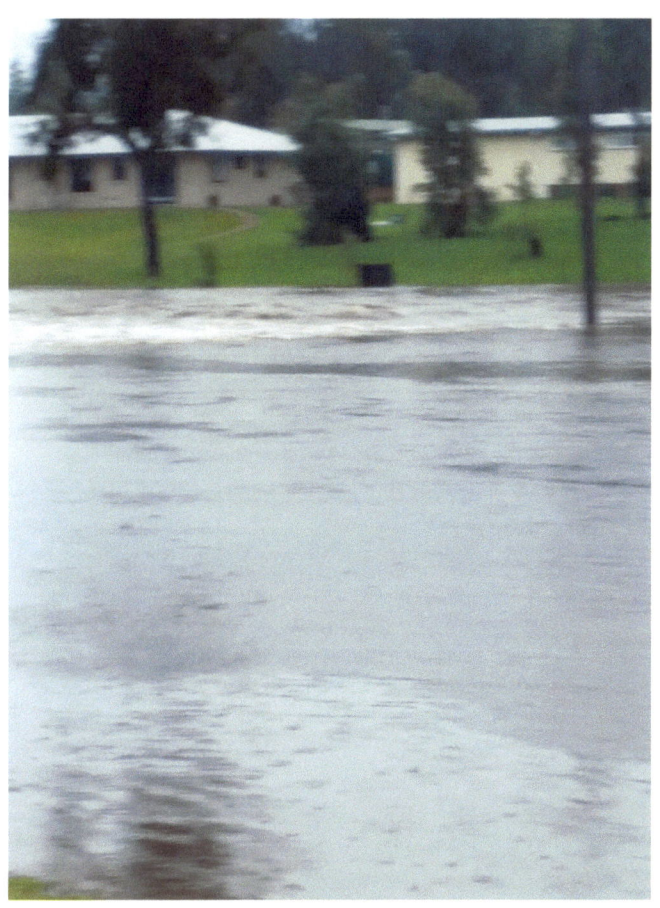
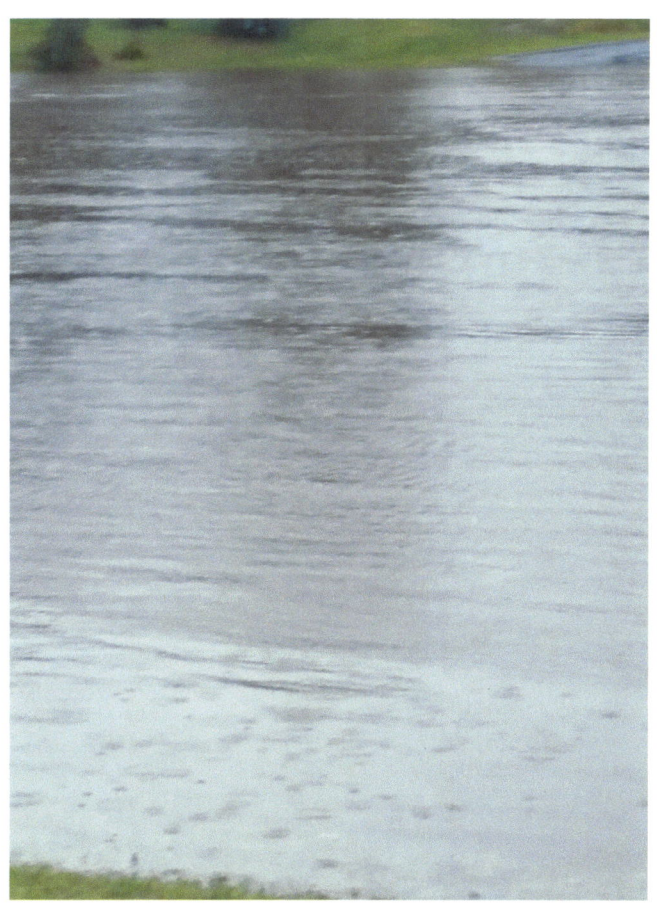
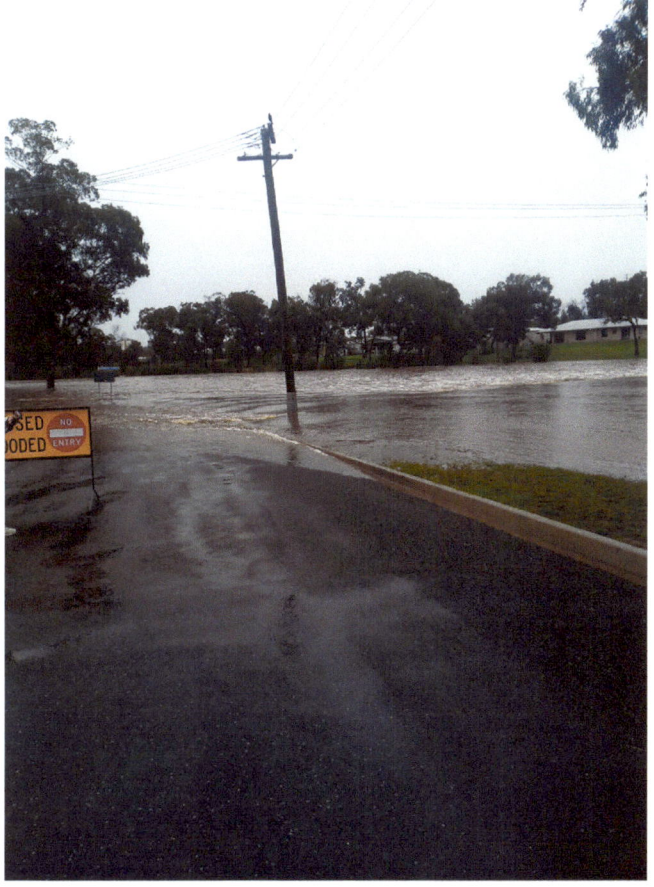
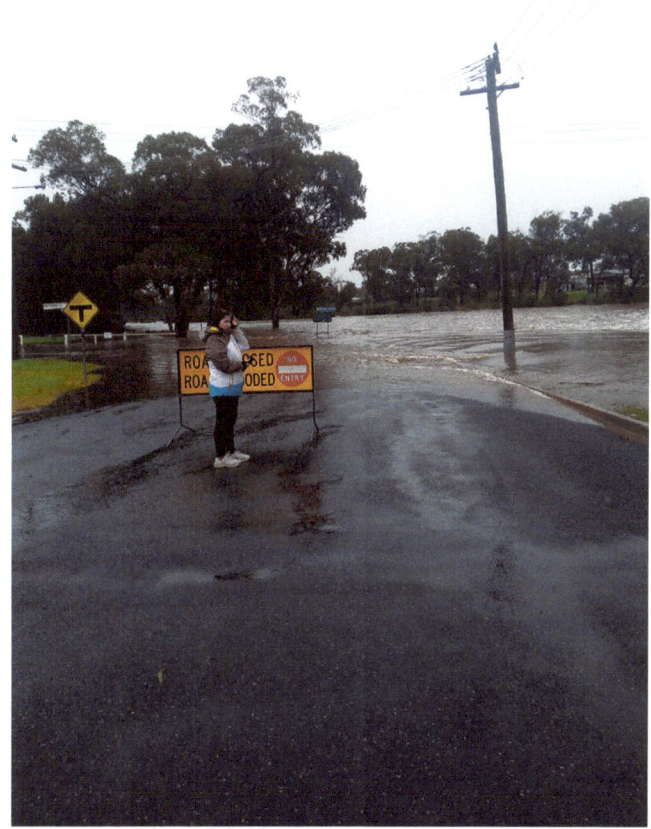

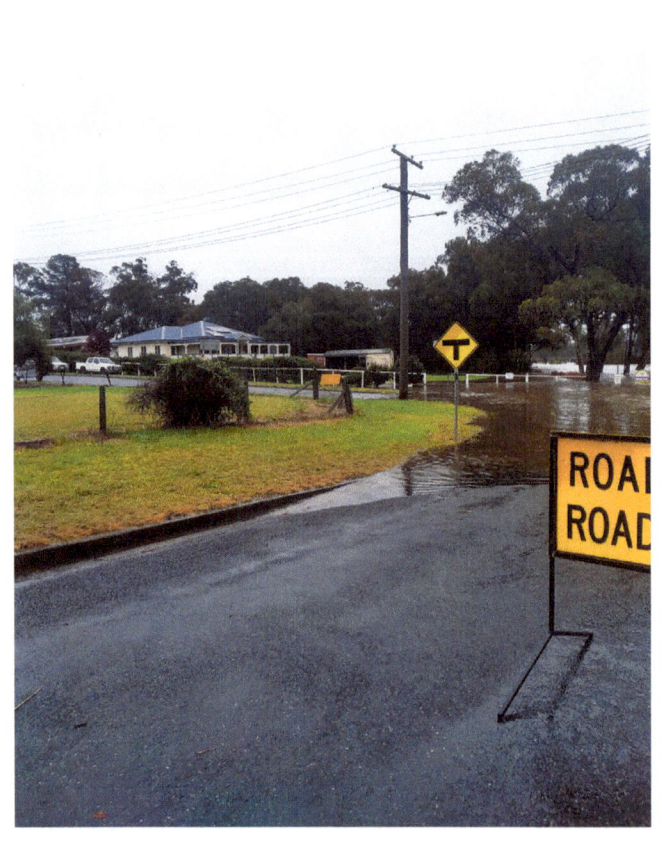
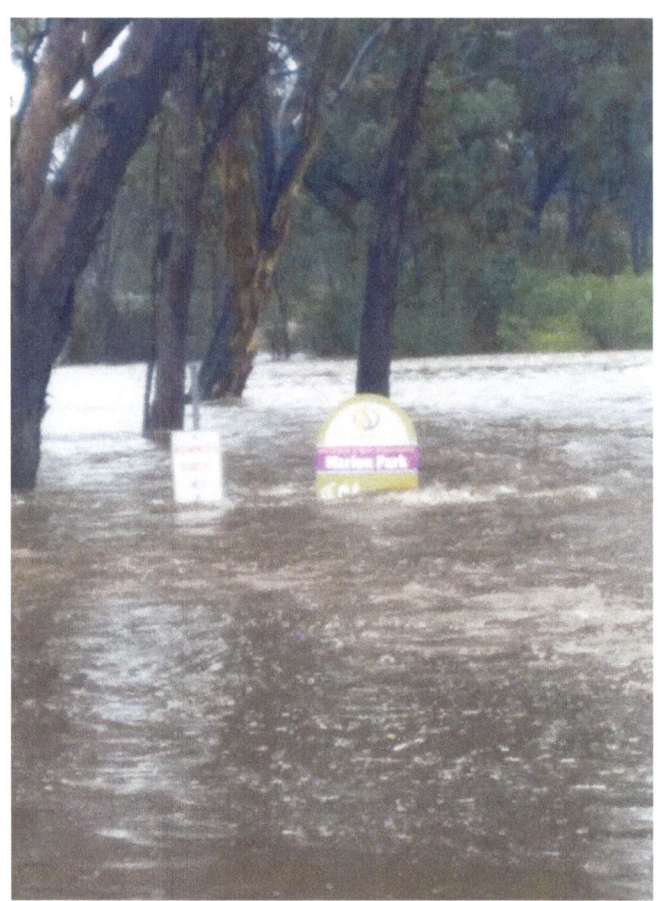
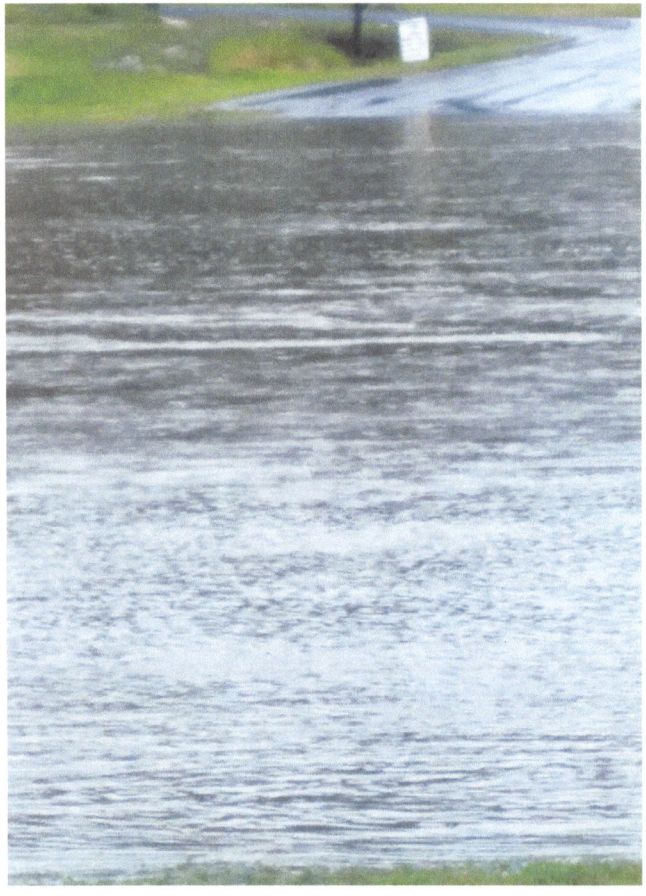
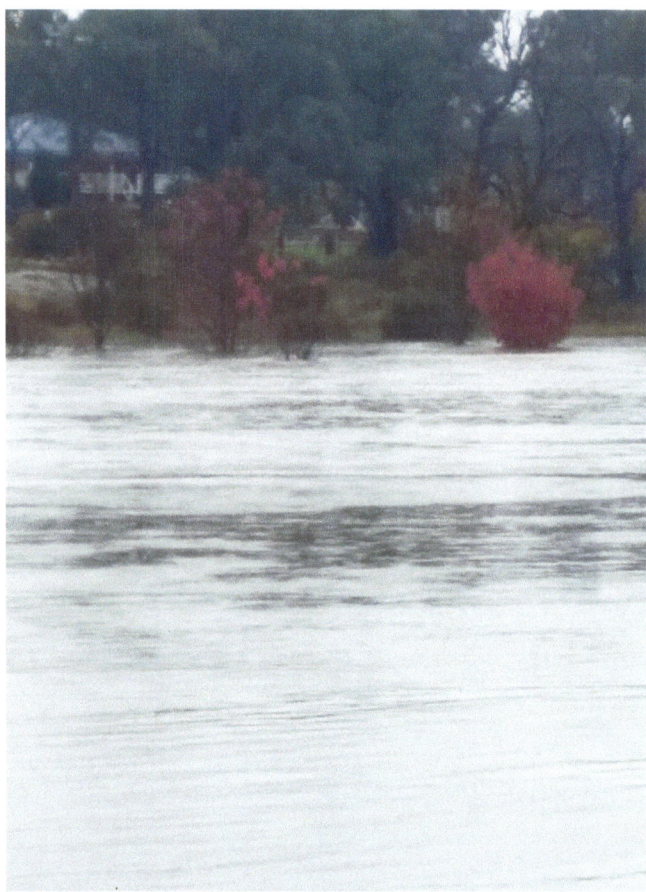

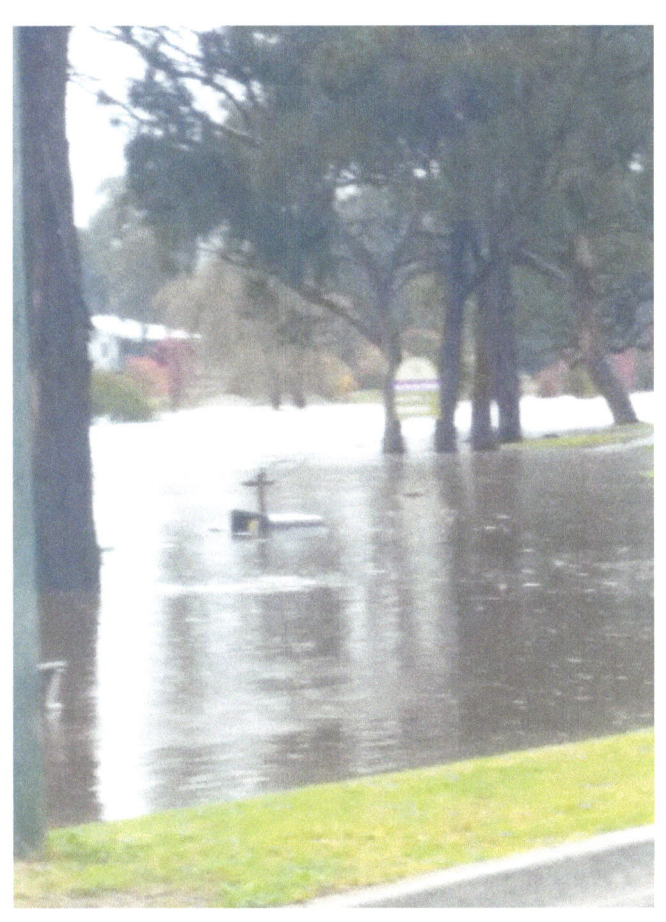
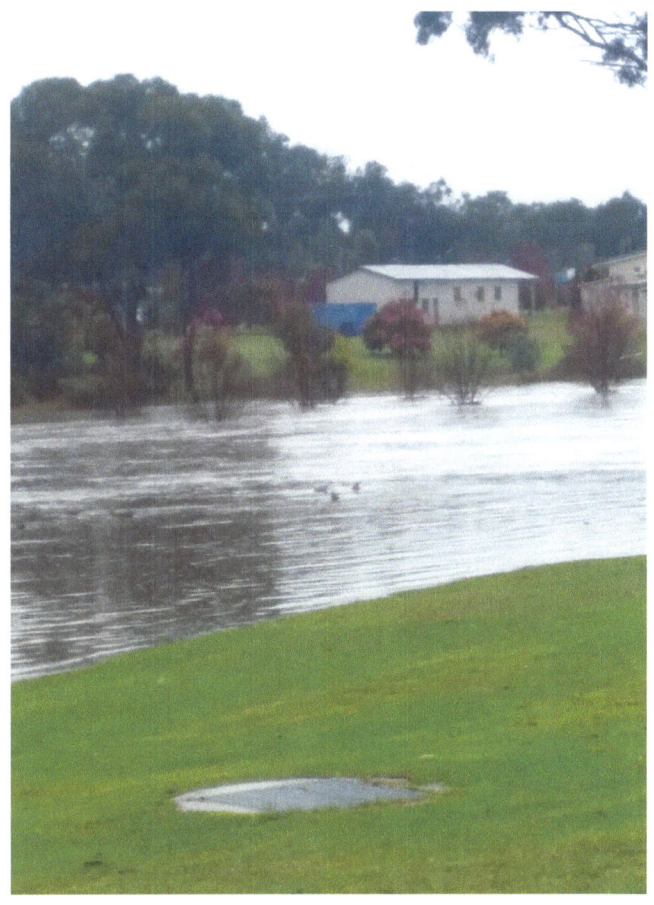
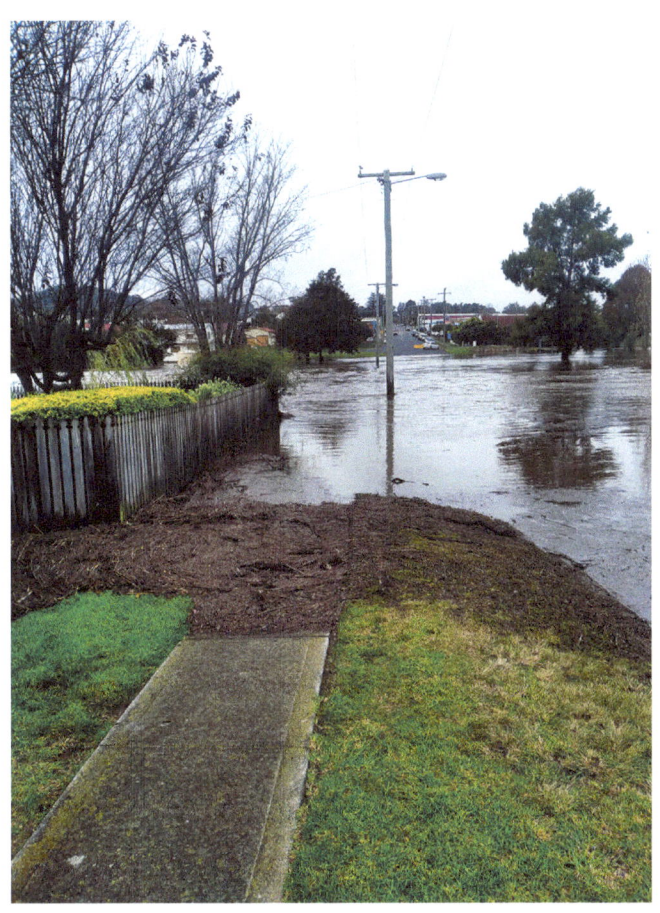
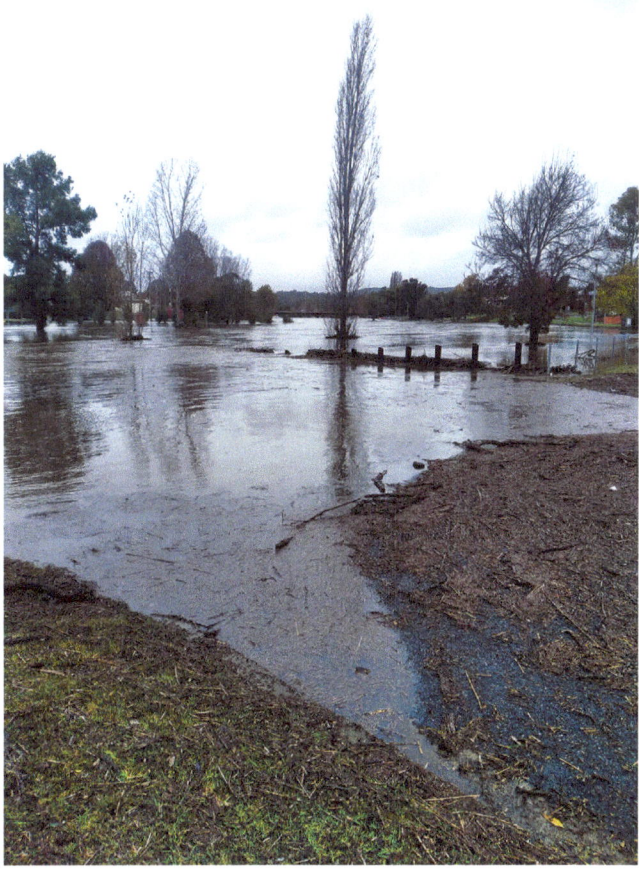

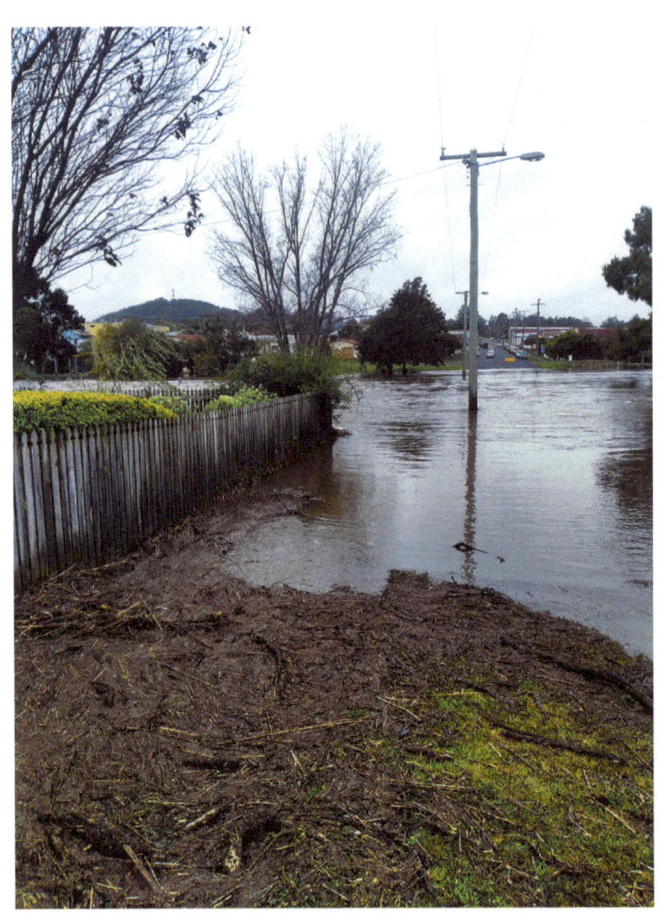
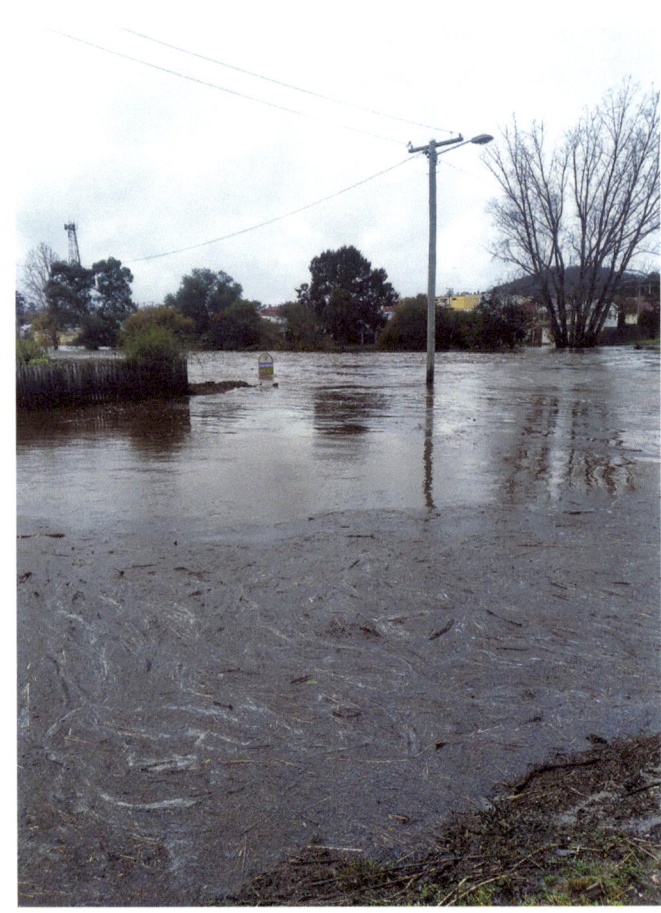
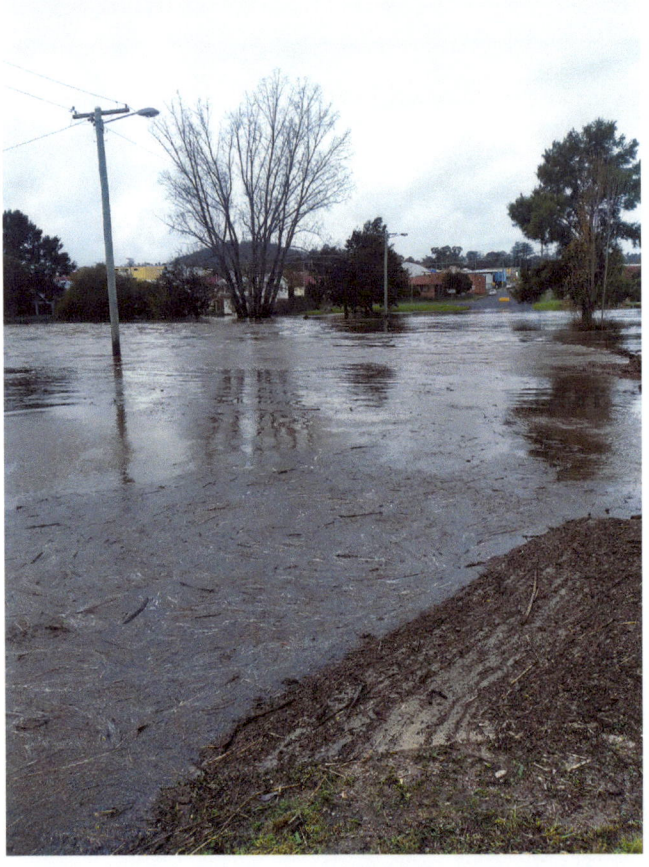
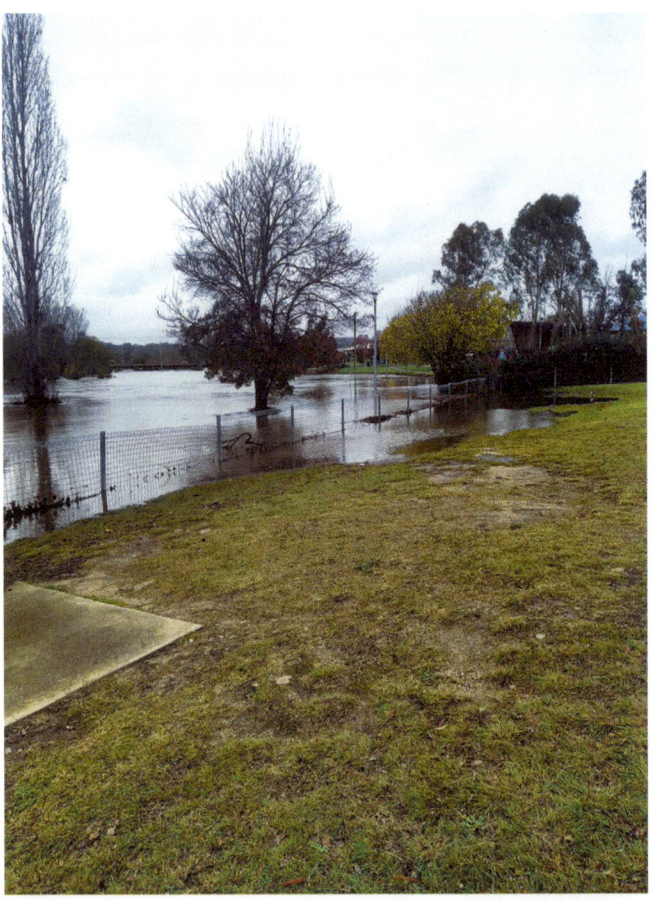

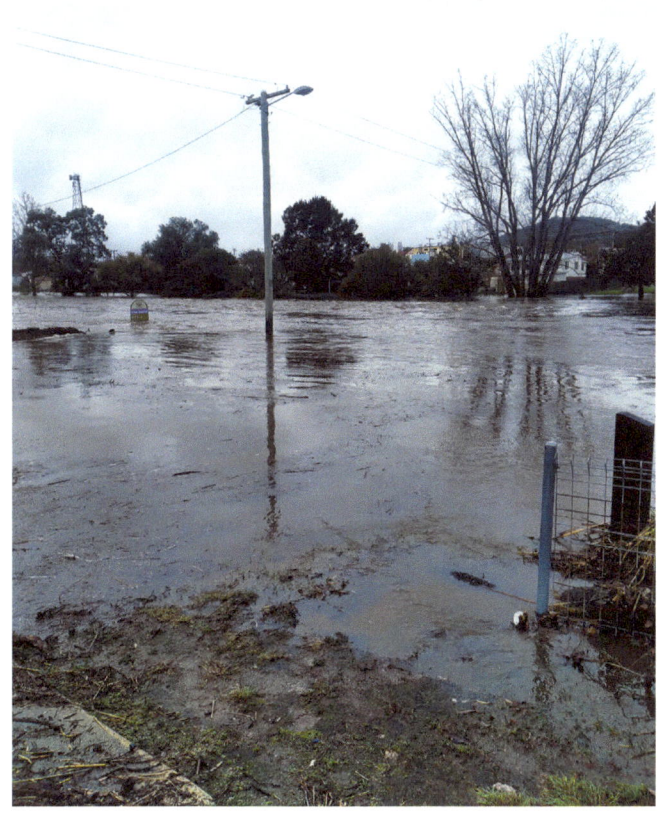
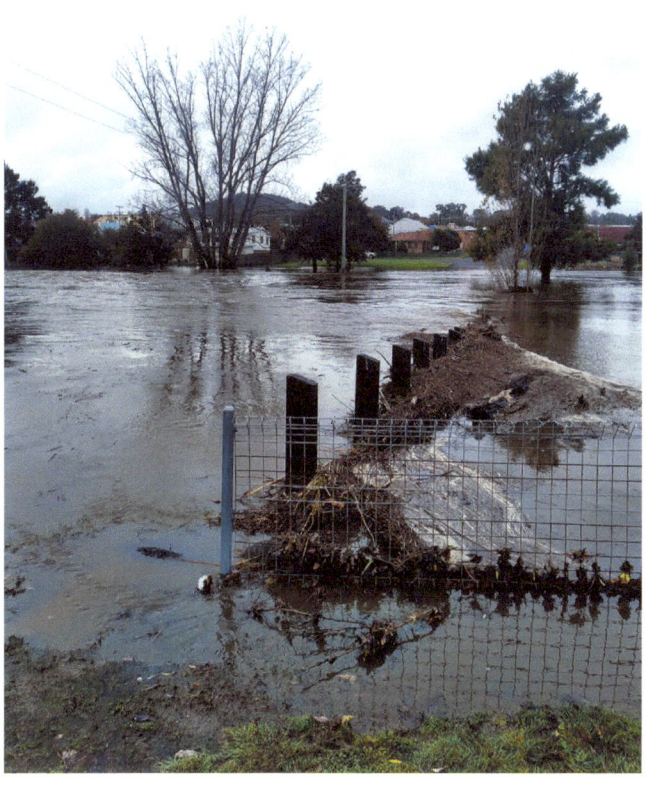
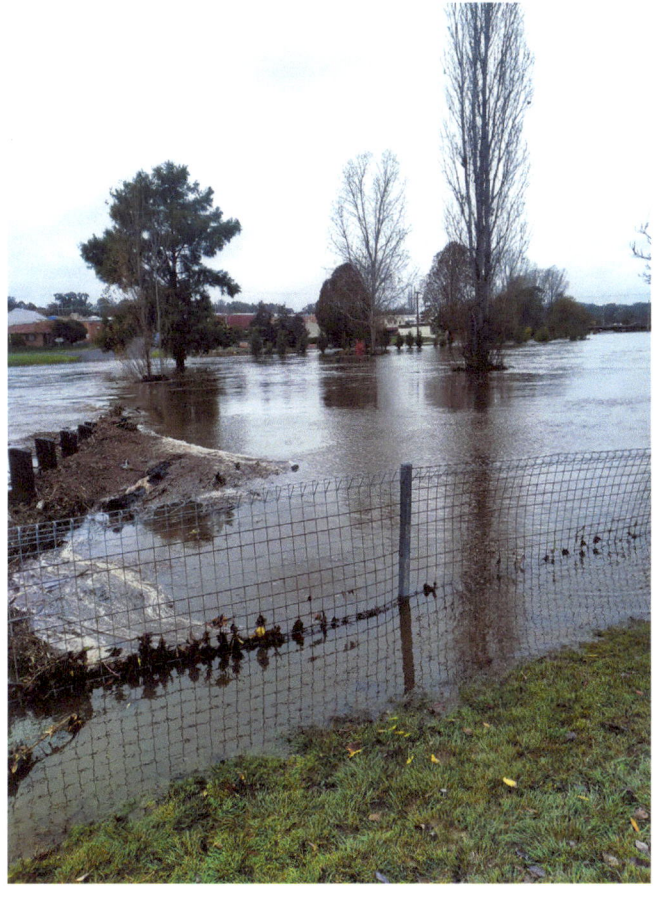
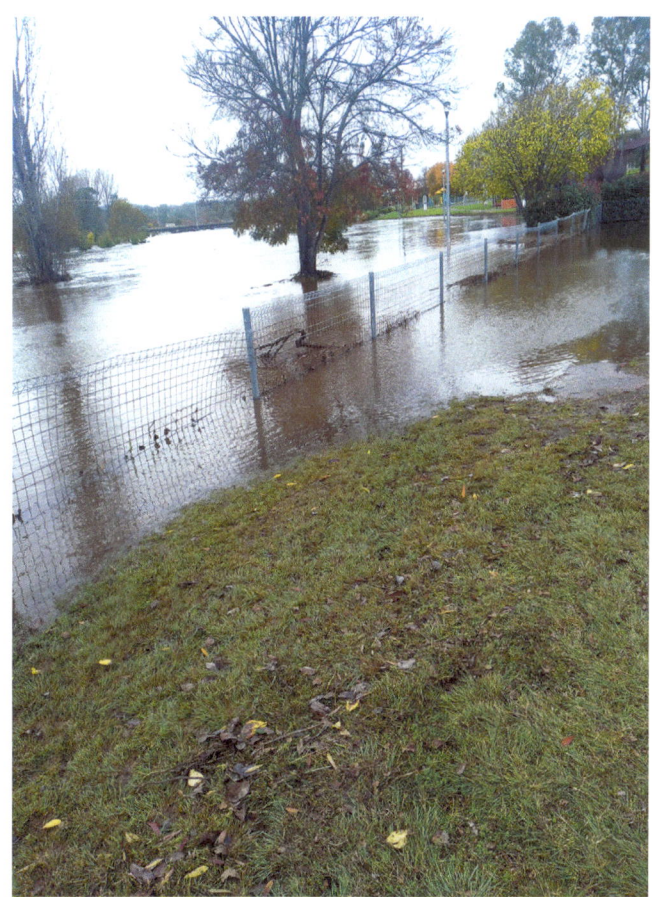

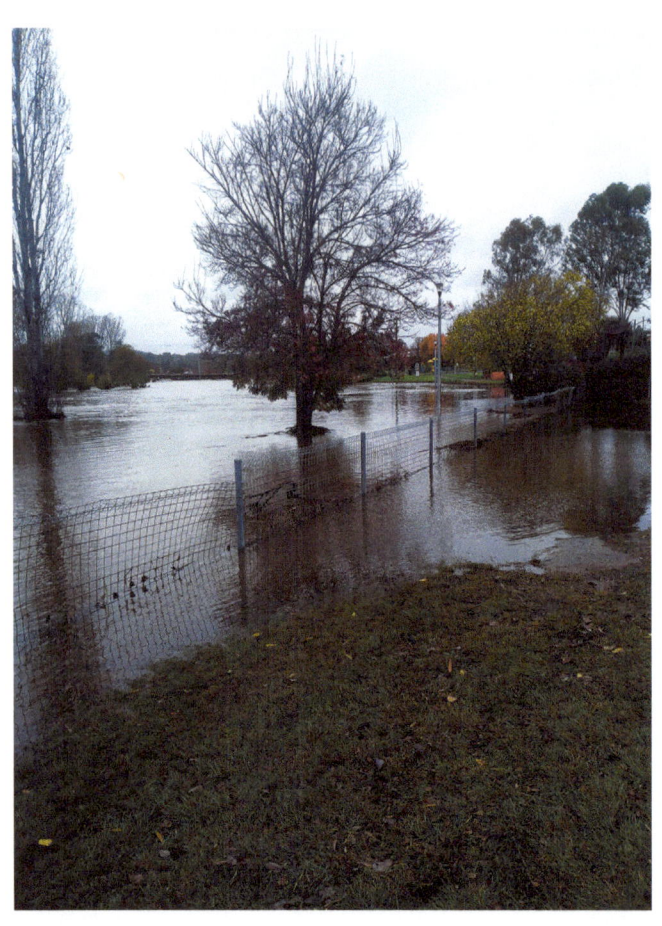
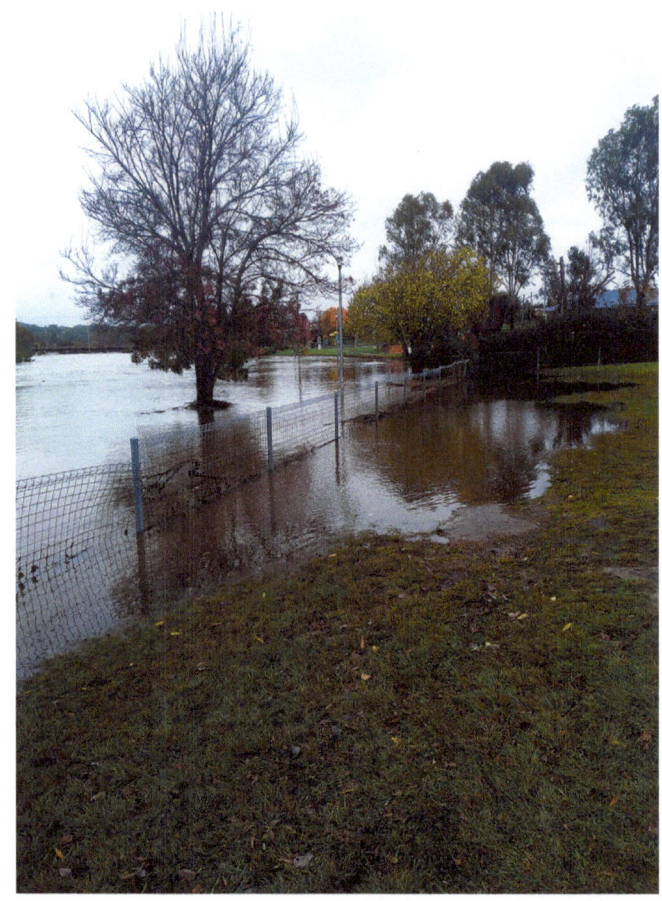
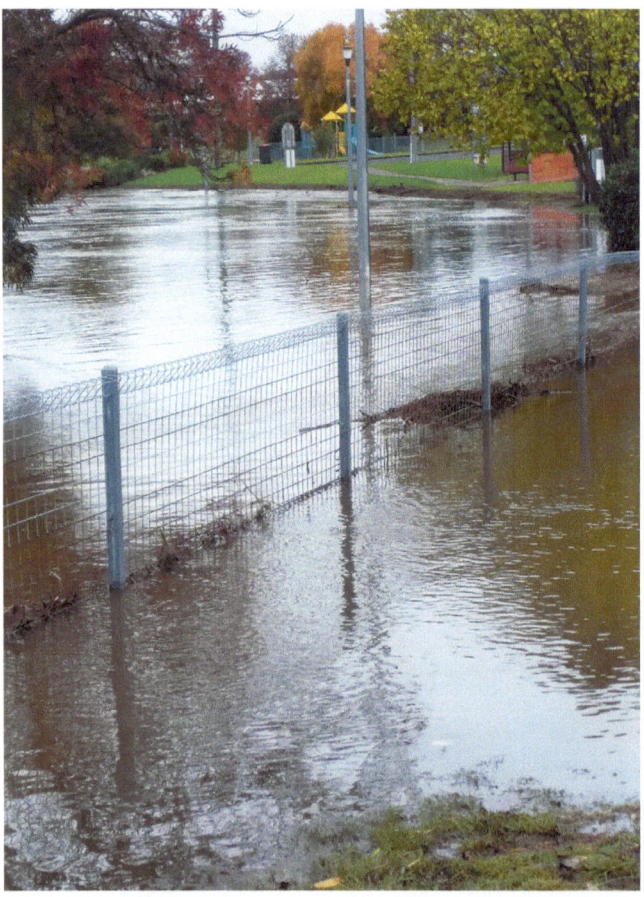
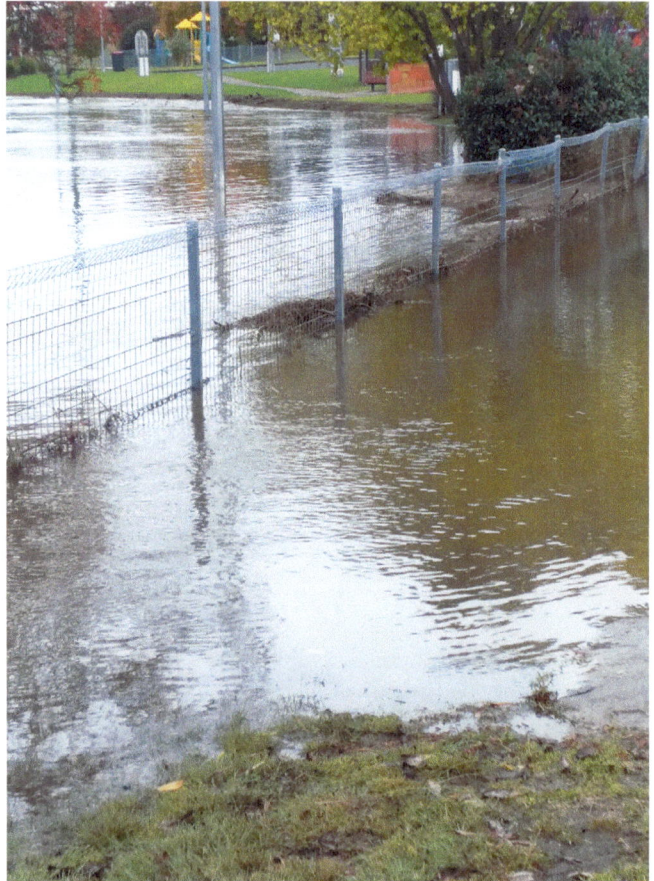

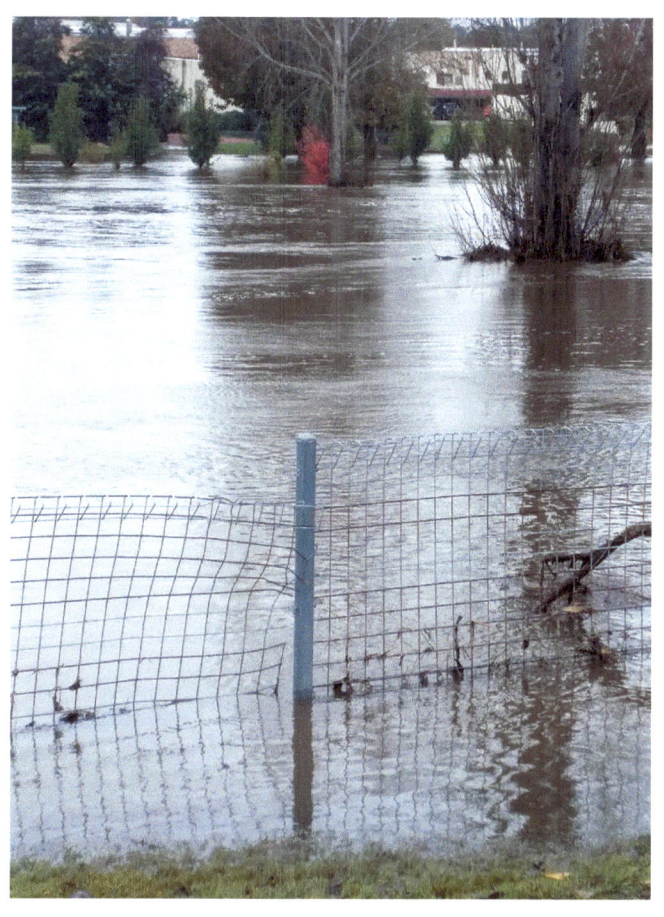
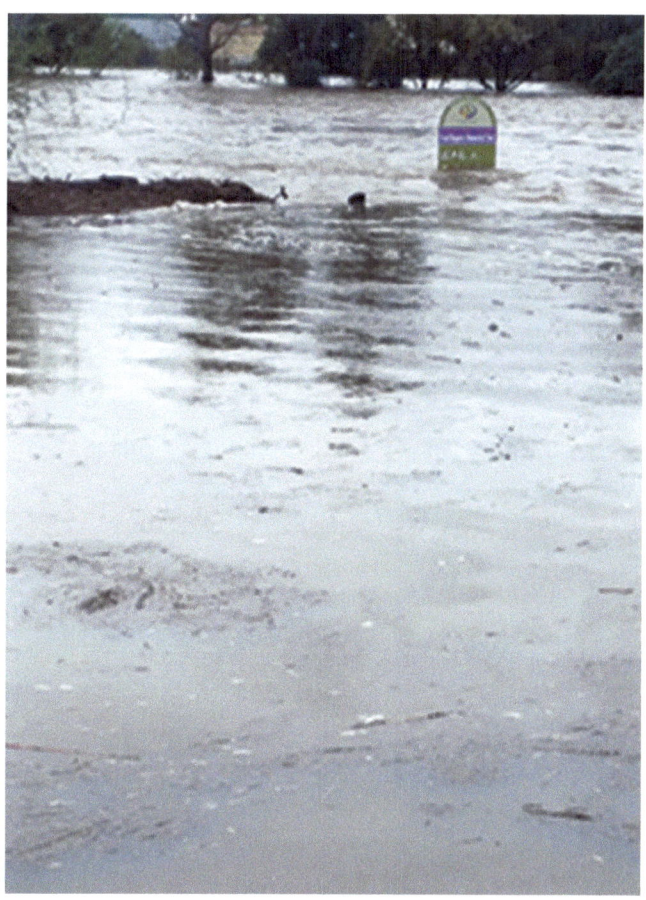
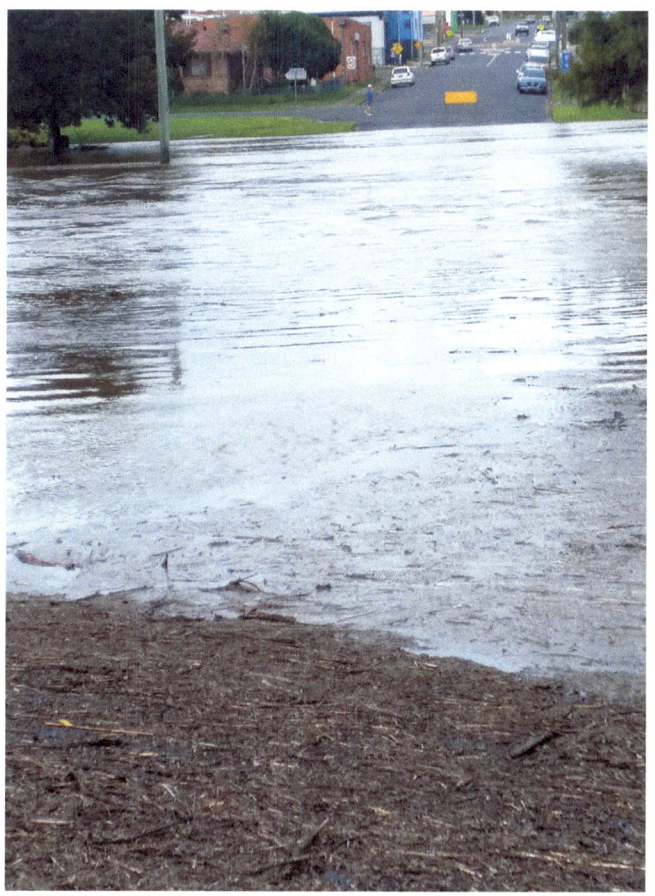
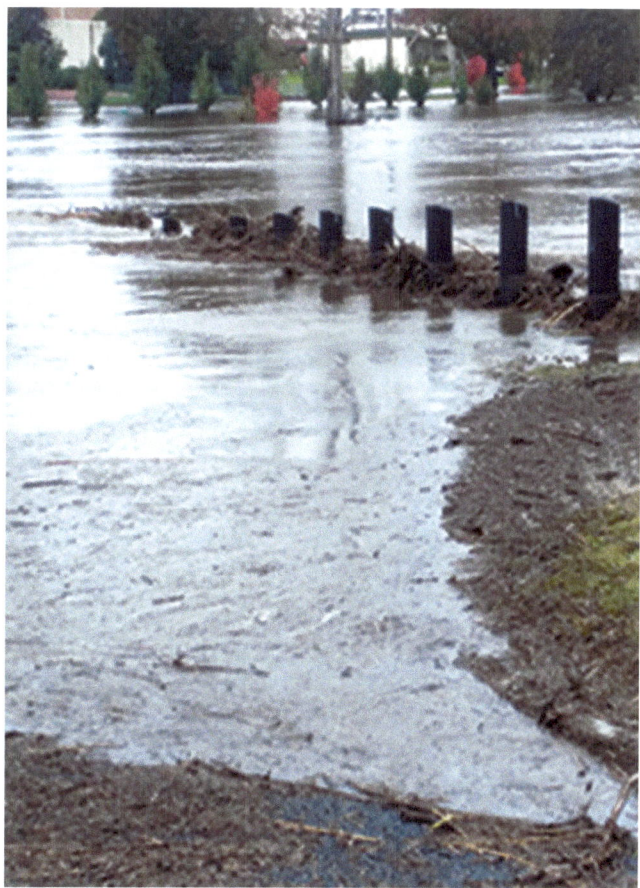

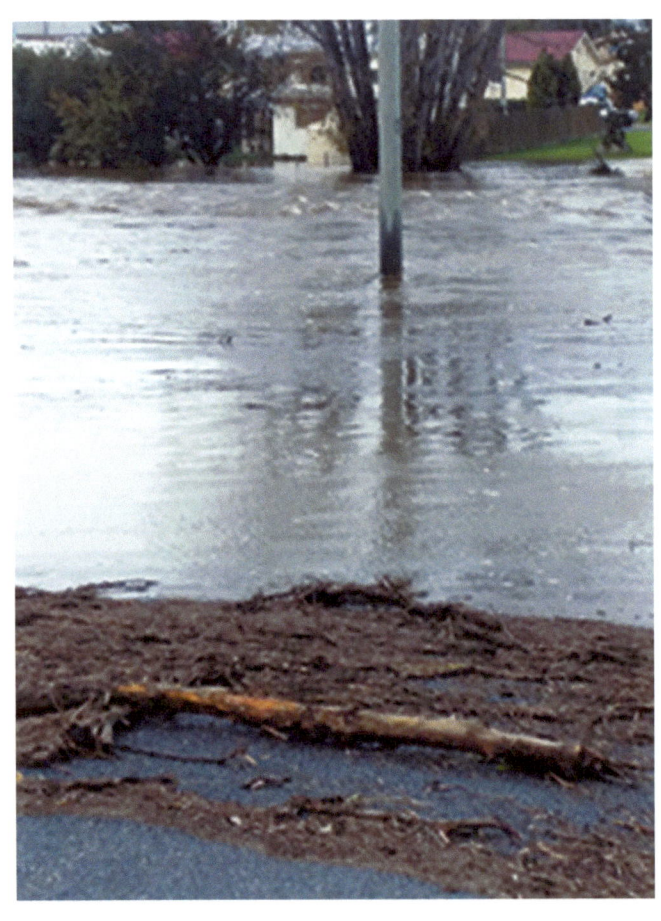
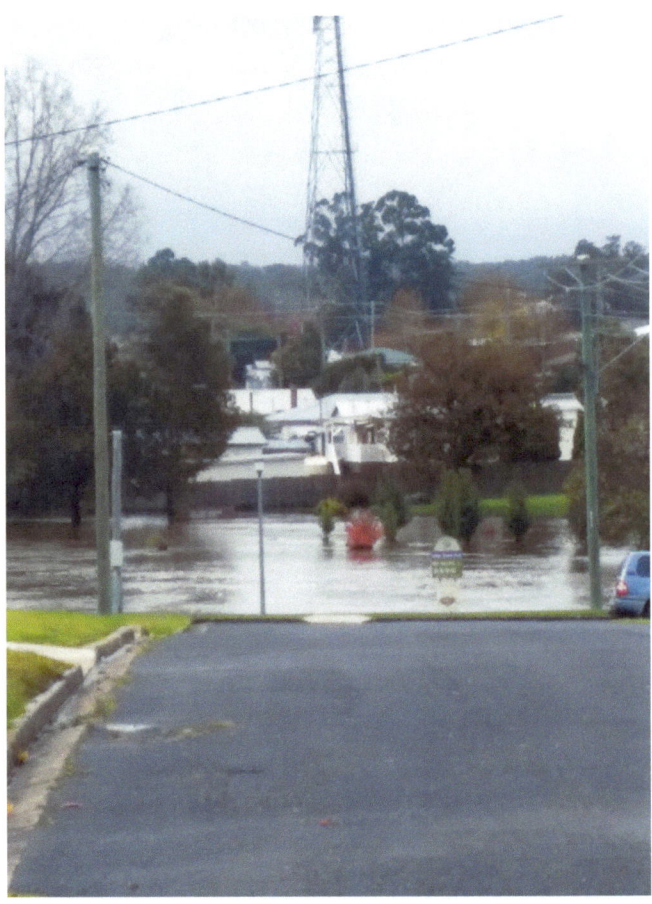
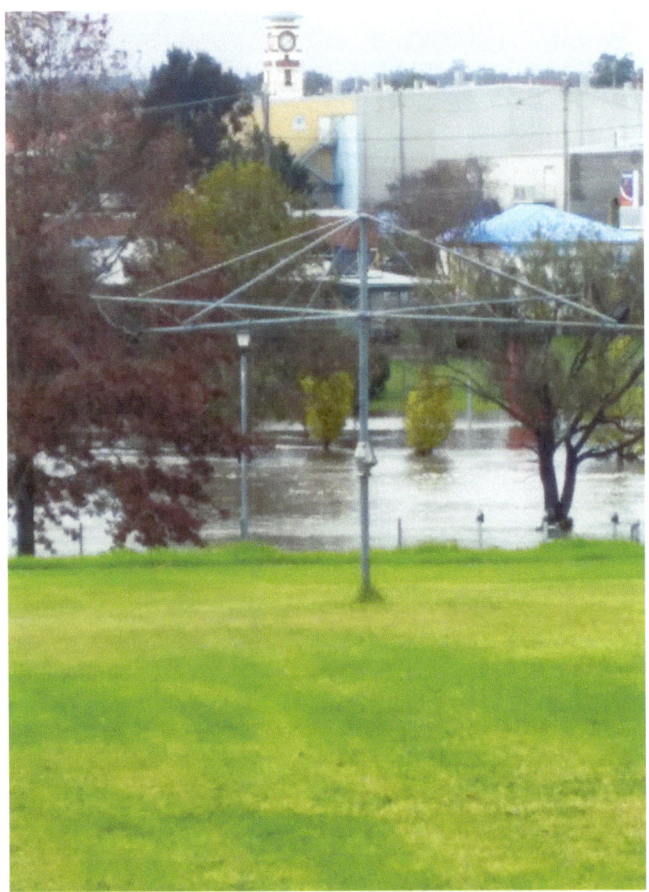
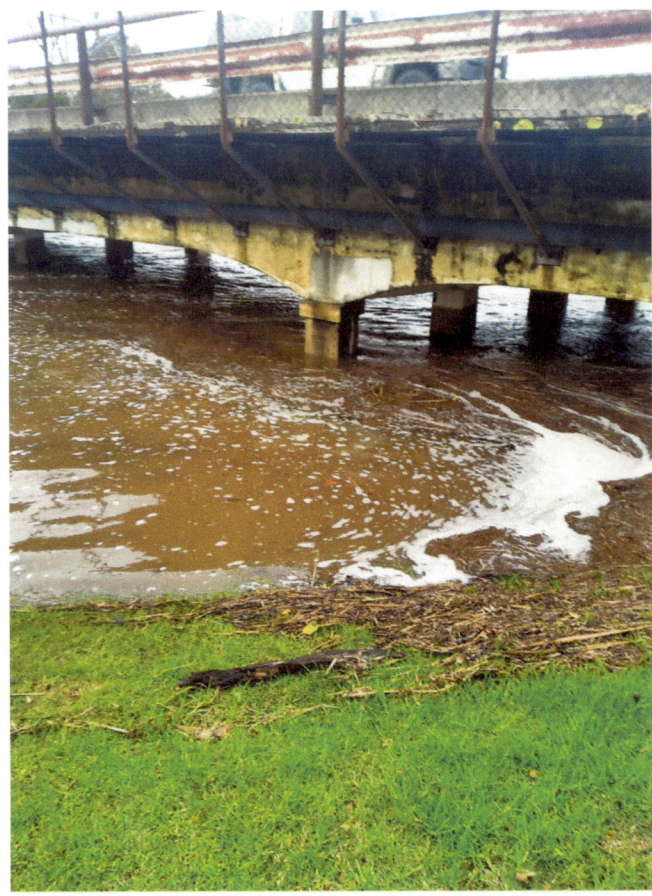

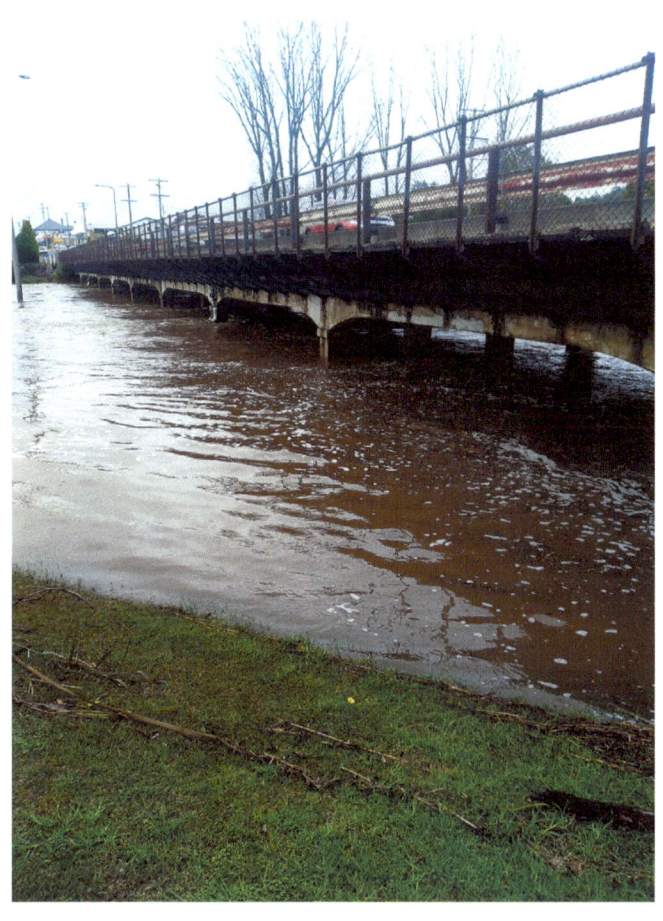
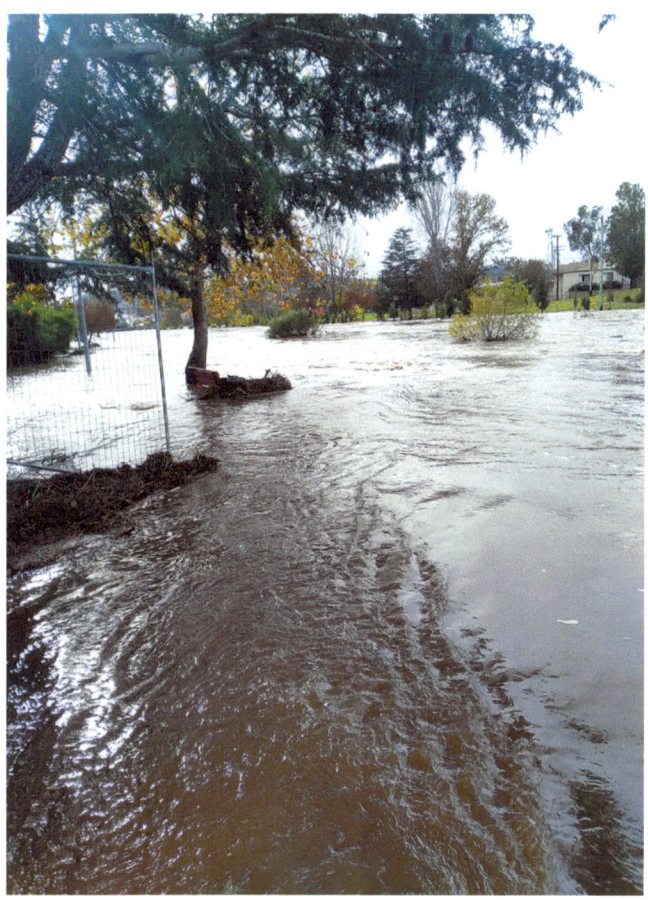
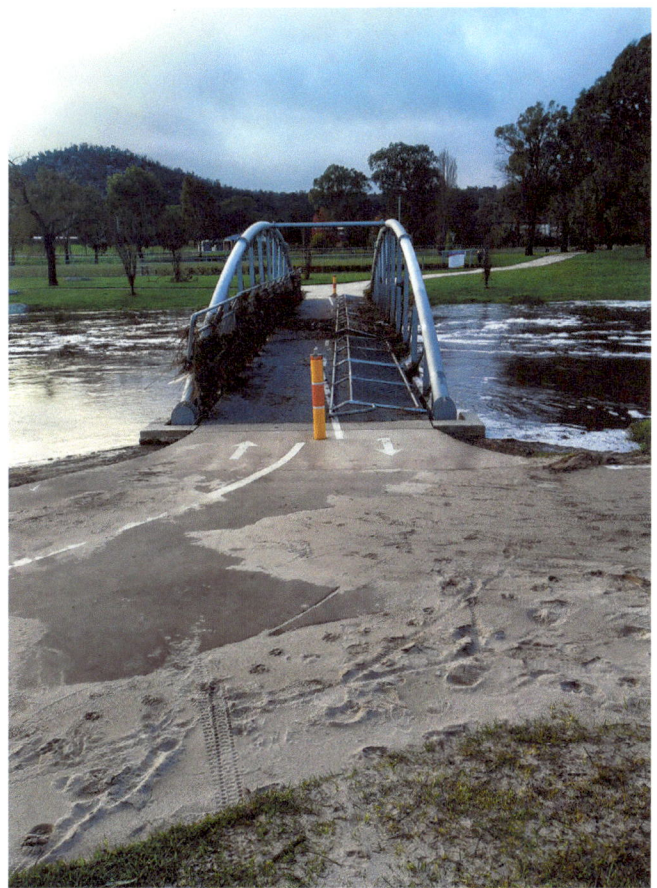
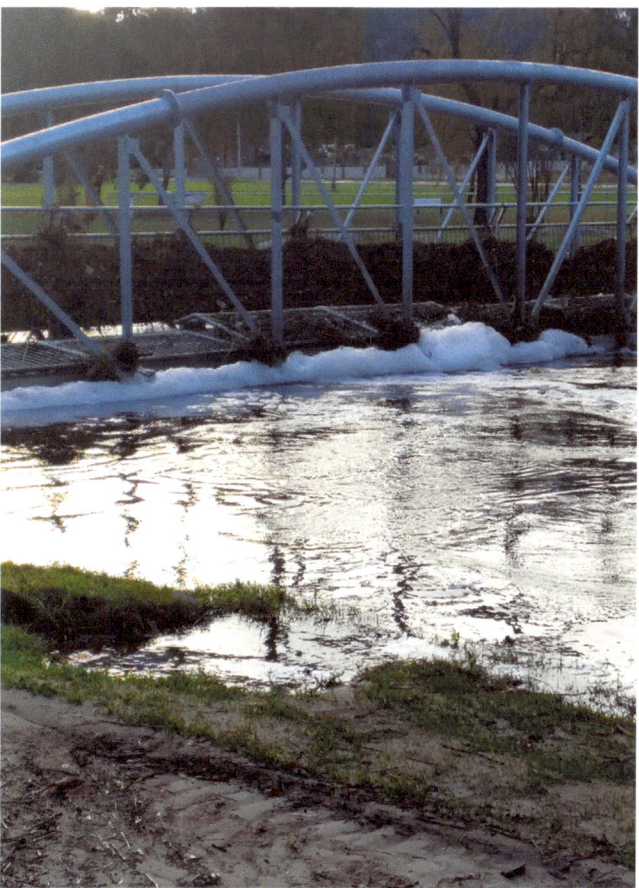

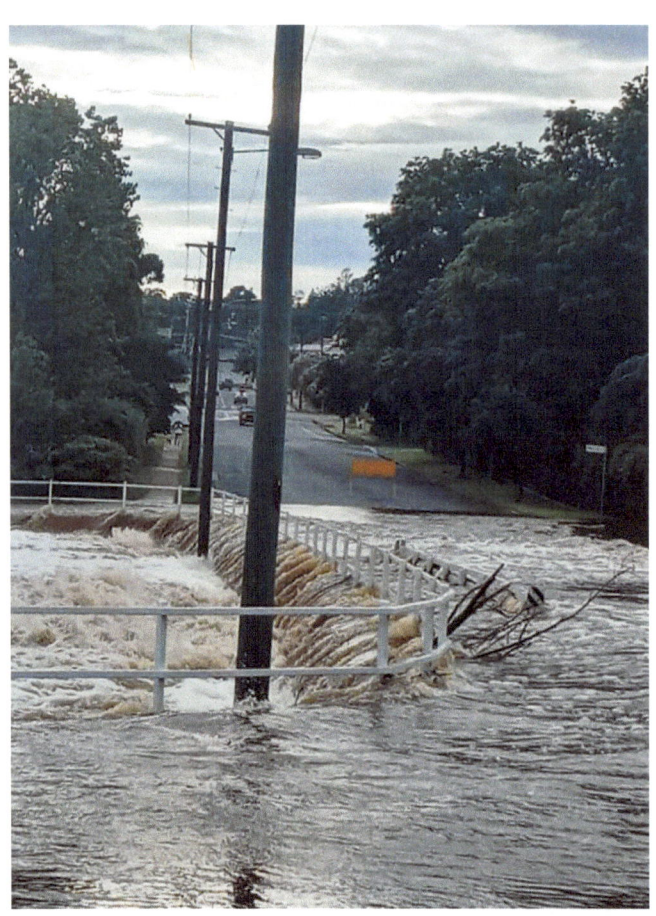
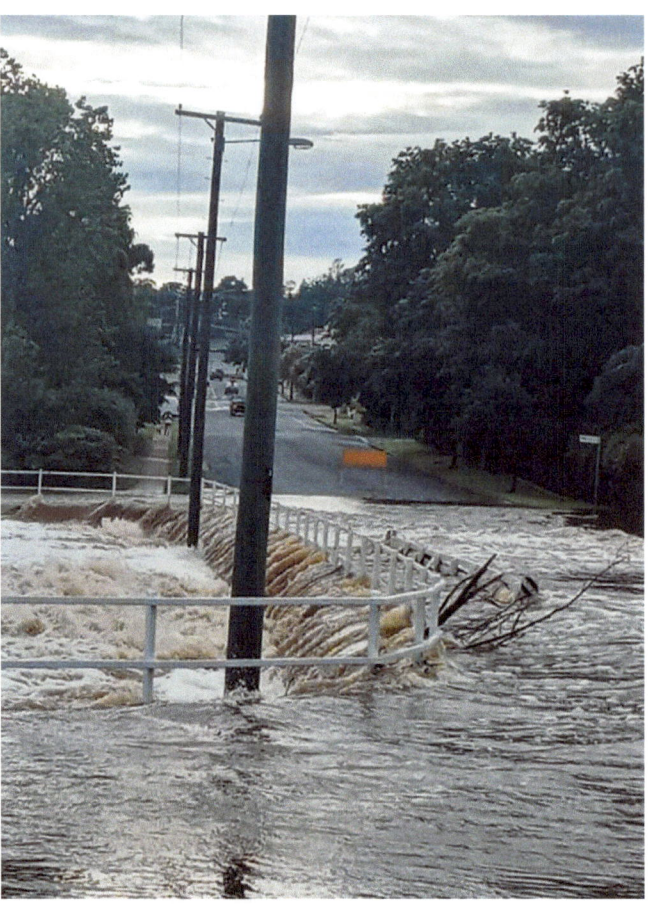
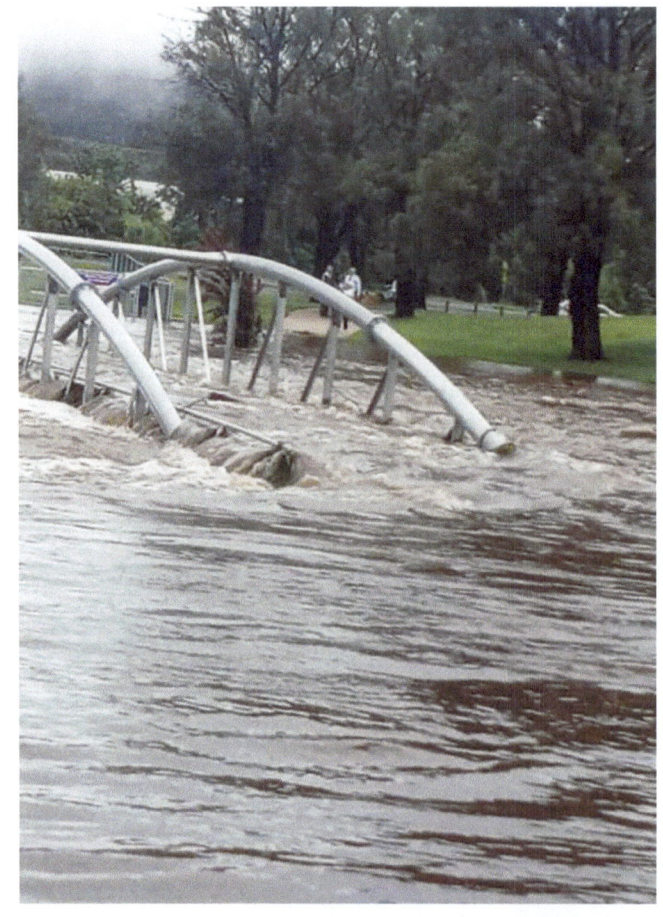

Floods 2022

It's flooding

Everywhere at once how insane

2022 floods are worst in history now

If it's flooded please don't be a fool

Showing of thinking your really cool

People are losing loved ones in the floods

The floods seem to come then go away and then it comes back in a day or two

The floods been coming back quicker than before

People have lost everything they own

Even special sentimental things

Sentimental things you can't replace

I know it's sad and very hard to lose everything you own

Especially your sentimental things which mean the world to you

But least your life was spared

And your still here today

And it's amazing seeing people helping each other as well

And helping each other restart their lives and start a fresh

And helping one another with any household things and clothes they need to

It's good to see the community reaching out helping those in need and all getting together for the big clean up after the floods

And to the parents who were rescued in the floods and then gave birth the same day congrats on the birth of the baby

The baby will have a story to tell when it grows up as well

Who would of thought the couple would of been rescued from the floods then have a baby on the very same day

Hope you are all doing well to

But to everyone else please becareful around flooded waters

Stay away from flooded waters if you can unless your one of the rescuers and have to give a helping hand

By Adelaide Meharg

www.ingramcontent.com/pod-product-compliance
Lightning Source LLC
Chambersburg PA
CBHW041935240526
45473CB00034B/1683